CLIMB HIGHER

HIGHER

PURSUE YOUR PASSION WITH PURPOSE

D1514453

PARTRIDGE

CLIMB
HIGHER

PURSUE YOUR PASSION WITH PURPOSE

MITCH LEWIS

WITH KEITH WALL

ISBN:	Hardcover	978-1-5437-4375-3
	Softcover	978-1-5437-4376-0
	eBook	978-1-5437-4377-7

Print information available on the last page.

To order additional copies of this book, contact
Toll Free 800 101 2657 (Singapore)
Toll Free 1 800 81 7340 (Malaysia)
orders.singapore@partridgepublishing.com

www.partridgepublishing.com/singapore

This book is dedicated to all those here who told their personal story, contributed to this book, and are helping to make the world a better place.

To our children: Jeremy, Nick, Jessica, Vincent, and Sadie; and our grandchildren: Leah Jo, Kailea, Ella, Jackson, and Clara Marie. You are all the light in our lives and give us hope and optimism for the next generation of humanity.

Moreover, to my beautiful wife, Michelle, collaborator in life, and without whom writing this would not have been possible. You bring joy, happiness, and compassion to everyone you know.

MITCH LEWIS is one of a very few people in the world to have run marathons on all seven continents and to have submitted the highest mountains on the same seven continents – the marathons after the age of 45 and the mountains after the age of 50. For more than three decades he has been an executive at such companies as AT&T, Ericson, Microsoft and Juniper Networks based in multiple locations in Europe, U.S., and in Asia. Mitch is a frequent speaker at corporate, community and special interest groups along with coaching and mentoring individuals and teams. He donates time and resources to cause-based organizations and people in need with the intention of helping to make the world a better place. He and his wife Michelle are the proud parents of five children and five grandchildren (with more on the way). They are in the process of relocating back to the Seattle area from Singapore where they have lived for the past four years.

KEITH WALL is a twenty-five year publishing veteran, has been an award-winning magazine editor, radio scriptwriter, and online columnist. Living in Colorado Springs, he currently writes full time with several bestselling authors.

"I have read Climb Higher and my spirit can't stop grinning."

- REV. DAVID BRUNER, Senior Minister & Spiritual Leader, Center for Spiritual Living, San Jose, California

"I have had the privilege of knowing my friend Mitch for over twenty years including 3 years we worked together in Stockholm for Ericson. As an industry executive and CEO, my highest priorities are formulating a compelling strategy and setting and driving results – however, nothing exceeds my priority of investing time and energy into building a high-performing and highly-motivated team that can manage through market changes. In his book, Mitch provides many strategies that resonate with me. I highly recommend that you read this book if you want valuable insights into how to be the best that you can be while improving results in your personal and professional lives."

- JOHN GIERE, CEO, Openwave Mobility

"As co-owner of Comlinx, an Information, Technology and Services company in Queensland, I partnered with Mitch for a number of years now to build our business in Australia. During this time, we've had a number of talks about how volunteerism and community service can help less fortunate people and leave the world in a better place for our children and grandchildren. Most of all, I appreciate our shared values and can endorse this book to help others who want to achieve extraordinary things in their lives..."

- WAYNE SHAW, Co-Owner, Comlinx, Brisbane Australia

"When I first contacted Mitch almost eight years ago, I was leading a search for a senior position at Juniper Networks. Juniper had a requirement that the candidate be an 'athlete' – not in the physical sense, but in aspects of agility, professional achievement and collaborative style. Never did I expect that this business athlete would climb Mount Everest the following year. Of all of my placements during the past decades, Mitch is one of my proudest when it comes to what he has accomplished as a professional and person. I would recommend this book to any 'athlete' wishing to drive results for their company, themselves and their teams."

- KATE BULLIS, Managing Partner, Go-To-Market Practice, SEBA International Executive Search

CONTENTS

FOREWORD

I first met Mitch Lewis in Punta Arenas, a small town in Patagonia, and the southern-most continental city in the world. Located at the tail end of the Andes, it is the gateway to the Antarctic and a popular place to see penguin colonies. Our goal was to climb Antarctica's Vinson Massif, 750 miles from the South Pole and the tallest mountain in the most remote and desolate continent.

As a CEO, I had just completed the sale of a leading strategy consultancy to KPMG, a global professional services firm. My career was taking a big turn, with an ambitious plan as the Global COO of Strategy for KPMG International. I set up three Strategy Centers for Excellence (in New York, London, and Hong Kong), established a network across the seventeen largest countries, and was delivering services to all major markets in the world. I sold my house in Toronto and used New York City and Hong Kong as home bases a few days a month while I travelled relentlessly around the globe. My life was mostly work, but I made some time for adventure.

Mitch and I stepped out onto Union Glacier from the Ilyushin, a Russian plane designed in the 1960s to carry large payloads and to land on short, unprepared airstrips in the worst weather conditions of Siberia and the Soviet Arctic. We set up our tent and waited for a weather window to make our way to Vinson.

Over the following two weeks, Mitch and I forged a deep relationship. We shared a rope as we navigated crevasses and climbed to the summit, enduring bitter cold, deep snow, and treacherous ice. We also shared stories, talking for hours each night huddled in our tent, aglow with the twenty-four hours of sunlight that beams in the Antarctic summer. I learned of Mitch's quest to be one of a select few in the world to complete a marathon as well as summit the highest peak on each continent.

Eventually, we stood atop Vinson, with the blistering wind and snow pounding our faces, arm-in-arm celebrating the completion of this amazing feat. Few things in life bond two people together like climbing a very high, very dangerous mountain in tandem.

The next year I would read about Mitch's harrowing adventures in his first book, *Climbing Your Personal Everest,* where he tells of being a forty-five-year-old coach potato, trapped in a mediocre life, who finally decides to take action and transcend from ordinary to extraordinary. In that book, Mitch shared how he conquered his fears and inertia to turn his life around—and compelled readers to learn from his story in the hope of having a lasting and positive impact on people who also find themselves stuck.

In this second book, *Climb Higher,* Mitch leads us through an emotional journey of hardship, heartache, perseverance, and ultimately, triumph. He neatly threads his own pilgrimage with brilliant stories of those he has encountered on his life path. These are all ordinary people who, when faced with daunting obstacles, rose to their unique challenges and took big leaps forward. I am sure you will find these deeply personal stories both enthralling and inspiring.

As Mitch was writing this book, I was going through my own hardship. Mitch refers to the Everest tragedy that occurred on April 18, 2014, when seracs—also known as ice ridges—failed on the western spur, resulting in an ice avalanche. Sixteen people lost their lives that day. I was on my own summit attempt at that time, and six people from my expedition perished. We were all in a state of shock while the search and rescue unfolded. It was a tragic loss for so many families.

Earlier that year, my relationship with a kind, lovely, and intelligent woman came to an end. She was pursing her career as a pediatric-orthopedic surgeon at a top research hospital in New York. Given her schedule and my travel, we rarely saw each other and grew apart—an outcome I regret to this day.

Toward the end of 2014, I endured a hardship of a different kind: I became a target for an extortion scheme. Fabricated accusations were quickly proved untrue—but only after I waited months for the legal system to get around to the case. In the meantime, I suffered immensely, not knowing how such a situation could possibly happen to me. Journalists jumped on the story and, in an instant, my reputation was under attack for all to see. Needless to say, the follow-up story regarding the facts of the case were of far less interest to the media.

As I worked through my challenges, I learned how vulnerable we all are to life's uncertainties. Sharing experiences is cathartic, and opening up often results in others sharing in kind. In this process, I discovered how many of us have incredible struggles that lie just beneath the surface of our everyday lives: a car crash that takes a loved one's life, a diagnosis of terminal cancer, or a deep betrayal by a spouse or business partner.

In 2016, I started a new company, vivovii, dedicated to helping individuals, teams, and organizations attain peak performance in pursuit of their purpose. We offer a blend of professional services, in-person coaching, and an innovative technology platform, all backed by credible research. It was tough for me to reset my path, but thanks to the efforts of an incredible global team, vivovii is growing quickly and serving a critical need in the market.

We have all been told to "live our passion" or some variation on that theme. It is a good and true message. What makes it hard to live out are all the obstacles and setbacks that inevitably crop up. Thankfully, there is help along the way to provide profound inspiration and practical information. One such source is this book, as Mitch Lewis offers us hope and guidance through his own insights and the profiles of individuals who have climbed on in their individual journeys. If you're ready to climb higher and leap farther on your own journey, keep reading and absorb the wisdom this book has to offer.

STEPHEN JONES

Toronto

A GIANT STEP TOWARD YOUR DREAMS

Anyone can do anything—or almost anything—he or she wants to in life. I believe this with all my heart. I am a passionate believer in the art of the possible and the vast potential possessed by each person.

If you are ready to pursue the next big *anything* in your life, you've come to the right place. There is no better time than *right now* to dust off your dream—the one that's been languishing on the shelf far too long—and summon all your courage and resources to make it a reality. Do you feel like the opportunity has passed you by or that the challenges are too steep? I hope to show you in the pages ahead that you are, at this very moment, poised and primed to take a giant step toward your dream. As the nineteenth-century novelist George Eliot wrote, "It's never too late to be what you might have been."

Most people reach the point in life where they feel compelled to *do* more and *be* more. Perhaps they redefine what is meaningful in life and begin investing their time in things that matter. Perhaps they realize they have been "stuck in a rut with a gut" and finally choose to do something about it. Perhaps they reach a milestone birthday or encounter a significant setback, and decide to pursue a grand ambition.

After I summited Mt. Everest, I came home to many people who said things like, "Congratulations! What you did is amazing, but I could never do that—or anything close." I would respond, "Thanks, but you really can achieve 'your own personal Everest,' whatever that might be, if you're determined and dedicated enough."

I'd ask these people about their cherished dream, something others might not know, and what is stopping them from going all out to achieve that dream. I heard all kinds of excuses and rationales, some legitimate and others unconvincing. This prompted me to write my first book, *Climbing Your Personal Everest*, to provide inspiration and information about setting a big goal and going for it. I shared what I learned about being a former middle-aged couch potato who became a marathon runner and mountain climber. The underlying message: If I can do something like this, so can you!

Through the process of telling my story, I achieved another one of my dreams: becoming a published author and hearing from many people who felt inspired to start running marathons, launch an organization, take up a musical instrument, or pursue love. Shortly after publishing that book, I married my sweetheart, Michelle, and accepted a job offer that took us to Singapore—a challenging role in a challenging environment. We have seen parts of the world we never thought possible and tried to make a difference in people's lives in places like Indonesia, Tibet, and Myanmar.

I became a grandfather for the first time and felt the sheer delight of having a baby girl melt my heart—and watching her melt my son's heart as well. I also started learning the keyboard so I could plunk out a few songs for her and perform at a corporate event (and in the process gained enormous respect for *real* musicians who master instruments and vocal skills).

Along the way, Michelle and I have both enjoyed the experience of living and working abroad, but also imagining and planning for our own inevitable transition from this phase of our lives. Believe me when I say I'm on the journey with you and share your fears and worries, as well as the excitement and exhilaration about the road ahead.

I became fascinated by other people's stories and the "magic moment" when they decided to make the next leap forward in their lives. How did they know it was time to move from one situation to another? How did they manage the transition? What challenges did they face? How did they persevere through setbacks? I can honestly say I still don't have all the answers (and never trust someone who says they do). But I've learned quite a bit from my own journey and, even more so, from the many people who shared their stories with me. I gleaned valuable insights as I explored how others went about the process of metamorphosis and transformation as they crawled, walked, or sprinted toward their dreamed-of finish line.

My own life has probably evolved somewhat like yours. I went to school, got married, had kids, bought a house, moved around, saved some money, and along the way lost friends, loves and—at times—hope for a better future. I was, and still am, confronting self-doubt and cultivating self-confidence. If you're at all like me, you've had a voice in your head saying that whatever you've done, whatever you've achieved, is not enough. Maybe you're aware of the relentless passage of time and realize that you are, in golf parlance, on the "back nine."

I remember when age thirty seemed old. Through luck, hard work, persistence, and the kindness and mentorship of many wise people, I think I've done more and seen more than could be expected from a short, lower-middle-class Jewish kid growing up in suburban Los Angeles. But the stark reality is that we only have so much time left to pursue our unrealized dreams, and I'm hungry to see what's next.

We are all familiar with Maslow's Hierarchy of Needs. We know that when the needs for safety and physiological well-being are satisfied, the next class of needs for love and belonging emerge. These are followed by the need for esteem.

As we move through the hierarchy and all of the preceding needs are satisfied, then and only then is the need for self-actualization activated. Maslow describes self-actualization as a "person's need to be and do that which the person was born to do." In essence, "A musician must make music, an artist must paint, and a poet must write."

These needs make themselves felt in signs of restlessness. The person feels on edge, tense, impatient, even irritable. It is not always clear what a person wants when there is a need for self-actualization. For many this comes about in trying to be an ideal parent, or in athletic achievement, artistic accomplishment, or even entrepreneurship.

Much later in life, after going through his own experiences, Maslow introduced the concept of "self-transcendence" – defined as "full spiritual awakening or liberation from egocentricity." He also defined it as selflessness and in giving of oneself to a higher goal in altruism and spirituality.

All of this brings us back to you and your quest to do something significant and meaningful. If you believe that Maslow was on to something, as I do, then you agree that your desire to fulfil your potential, leave a legacy, and contribute to something bigger than yourself is much more than "chasing after a crazy dream" or an attempt at self-aggrandizement.

Before I climbed Everest, I thought standing on top of the highest point on our planet was equal to self-actualization and self-transcendence. Not exactly. That experience may have gotten me closer to fulfilling my potential, but the accomplishment was not the be-all and end-all. It was something I did, but it didn't define who I was. It wasn't until much later, after descending the mountain, both literally and figuratively, that I realized our purpose for living on earth is more than a single accomplishment.

Our growth as human beings is a lifelong process, and our reason for being here needs to be continually clarified. A big part of my message in this book is challenging ourselves to define our own higher purpose and giving of ourselves to others so they can also grow.

The best-selling book *When Breath Becomes Air* is a powerful look at a stage IV lung cancer diagnosis through the eyes of a neurosurgeon. When Paul Kalanithi is given his diagnosis, he is forced to see this disease and the process of being sick as a patient rather than a doctor. The result of his experience is not just an examination of what living means from a scientific perspective, but also the essence of what makes life matter. When your own death is imminent, you're likely to become highly motivated to explore the meaning of life.

Dr. Kalanithi had only twelve to eighteen months to live, while most of us believe and hope we have many decades left to live and make something of our short existence. As Dr. Kalanithi expressed, "Time for me is double-edged: every day brings me further from the low of my last cancer relapse, but every day also brings me closer to the next cancer recurrence—and eventually, death. Perhaps later than I think, but certainly sooner than I desire."[1]

We might know in the rational part of our brain that things don't always go as planned and, indeed, we are all going to die someday. We, and only we, are largely in control of our lives, and we have to find kindness, generosity, and the beauty around us, even during the darkest times. We have to love deeply and spiritually, living in the present.

Moreover, we have to find *what* we love and *do* what we love. We must align our actions with our priorities and passion to find meaning and purpose while constantly reassessing our path and progress.

The book in your hands provides guidance for this process and suggests steps toward your transformation—whether you aim to climb your own personal Everest or just become a better person. My hope is that you will be inspired to live with purpose as I highlight real-life individuals who have toiled and prevailed.

In the pages that follow, you will meet a number of fairly ordinary people like you and me who have done extraordinary things in their lives. These men and women candidly share what prompted them to take a courageous leap toward realizing their dreams. They outline how they overcame their own self-doubts, leveraged their support networks, and what they learned that can equip others to fulfill their own ambitions.

As I conducted research for this book, I also spoke with friends and strangers who were on a different path. These are folks who, after sixty-five or so years, decided to "hang up their boots" and travel a bit, read a little, fix up their house, take leisurely naps, binge-watch TV series, improve their golf game, and spend time with their grandchildren. God bless them. There's nothing at all wrong with this approach—it's their reward for working tirelessly during their long careers. It's a time for many to kick back and enjoy their golden years.

If, however, you're like me and want to be energized every day toward a really hard and important goal, this book is for you. I am writing for those who want to participate in the game—rough and tumble as it is—rather than spectate from the sidelines.

We've used the phrase "ordinary people achieving extraordinary things," which may sound simplistic or trite. But there's nothing simple or cliché when the descriptions aptly apply to actual individuals—people much like you— who have overcome hardships and conquered fears on their way toward achieving their vision. The following stories will help prove that someone just like you or me can follow their dreams to places they never thought possible.

Consider what you want your legacy to be and how you can make a difference in others' lives while achieving things you only dreamed about. Getting from here to there won't be easy, but accomplishing something of value never is. If you're ready for the next big leap forward in your life, this book will provide the inspiration and role models to empower you to do it.

Your fellow traveller on this journey,

MITCH LEWIS

CHAPTER 1

TIME FOR A NEW TRAJECTORY

End Your Unhelpful Inertia
and Gain Momentum in Another Direction

*"Even if you are on the right track,
you'll get run over if you just sit there."*
Will Rogers

Step back with me for a moment to high school science class. You recall that Newton's first law of motion states, "An object at rest stays at rest and an object in motion stays in motion with the same speed and in the same direction unless acted upon by an unbalanced force." Objects tend to "keep on doing what they're doing."

In fact, it is the natural tendency of objects to resist changes in their state of motion. This phenomenon is called *inertia*. But what is meant by the phrase *state of motion*? This refers to an object's velocity—the speed it travels in a certain direction.

So why are we talking about Isaac Newton in a book about pursuing your passion with purpose? Just substitute "objects" for "person," and it translates to "people tend to keep on doing what they're doing." An object (or person) at rest has zero velocity—and will remain with zero velocity in the absence of an "unbalanced force."

Objects in a state of rest stay at rest. People in a state of rest stay at rest. People tend to resist changing this state of motion or their own development unless action is taken.

The majority of people continue on the same path, with their own inertia, doing things the same way, because it's familiar and comfortable. Making the leap to a new adventure requires someone to shake off inertia and move into change with determination. You have to use your own energy and human potential to make this change. Just as the earth exerts a gravitational pull on everything from the ocean tides to the moon, our own current state of being, our mind, our surroundings, and the stories we tell ourselves exert a heavy-weight pull on what we believe we can or cannot do.

All the Right Moves

More than two centuries after Newton advanced scientific knowledge, Albert Einstein said, "Nothing happens until something moves." We all understand this well as we try to balance safety, security, and stability with constant change. Not making a change is far easier than changing, especially since we are wired for Maslow's Hierarchy of Needs to first have food, shelter, and safety. Thankfully, most of us in the developed world enjoy a decent job, safe surroundings, and supportive friends—but we also have a burning desire to do more, be more, achieve more.

What we think is safe and secure is not necessarily so. We can't wait for the change to happen to us—we have to take control of the trajectory of our lives. It's like jumping into a pool: The water is very cold at first and a shock to the system, but our dive carries us forward. Then we have to swim, breathing and paddling, keeping steady and straight. Why? Because the alternative is drowning.

A friend told me recently that in a few decades hardly anyone will *have* to work anymore. While I don't totally agree with this when I consider service industries, for example, we can already see the effects of manufacturing jobs being eliminated by robots and software industries. In the future, people will want to work at something that is both fulfilling and helps to make the world a better place.

I personally understand very well about inertia. When I was eighteen, I had the mistaken view from my parents' generation that I should find a job in an industry where I could work for thirty years, put money aside, and retire comfortably. I thought either the gas, electric, or phone-company would be a good choice for my three-decade career. I happened to have a girlfriend whose mother worked for the Bell System, so I got hired there. A few years later, at the ripe old age of twenty-two, I told my Uncle Richard that I wanted to get my proverbial gold watch in twenty-five years. His response stuck with me: "So what are you going to do then, when you're so-called 'retired'?" I looked at him blankly and couldn't think of anything to say. But I remember thinking, *I'll be happy. Won't I?*

About ten years later, after I'd advanced in the Bell System and after the 1984 break-up of the company, I was offered an early retirement package and buyout. I took a chance and moved to a small late-stage technology company doing early fiber-to-the-home developments—long before there was an Internet to drive data or video bits. I was scared and apprehensive but thought I was young enough (thirty-two) that I could still do something different if it didn't work out. If I had not made that move and changed my inertia, I would have stayed pigeonholed—stuck—in the same company, same position, and same geography. I would never have been able to enjoy the experiences and growth opportunities I've had since.

About five years after I joined the tech company, and after moving to the start-up's headquarters to lead account management, it was acquired by the Ericsson Corporation. This purchase led to all of the companies, countries, and roles that subsequently came to me. The world opened up to me—figuratively and literally, as I have been fortunate to have lived in several different countries and travelled to dozens more.

Valuable Frienemy

Inertia can be both your friend and enemy—just like the saying, "Keep your friends close and your enemies even closer." We have to embrace, nurture, and feed inertia so it will work for us instead of against us. We can alter an unfulfilling trajectory and gain momentum in a new, positive direction. So how do we control our inertia?

We have to acknowledge that there are indeed things we can control and things we can't. Some things are largely out of our control, including the stock market, economy, weather, health crises, or the political environment. However, we can reclaim some control if we set the course, while keeping our True North always in sight through the metaphorical small window in our ship.

5 —

Inertia can be a good thing. You can pick up speed along the way that propels you forward—if you are controlling and steering your ship. Then momentum begins to build. You will sometimes experience stretches in life when it seems like everything is going right. Your constant visualization of where you want to be versus where you don't want to be can build the right inertia.

In *The Catcher in the Rye*, J. D. Salinger wrote, "This fall I think you're riding for—it's a special kind of fall, a horrible kind. The man falling isn't permitted to feel or hear himself hit bottom. He just keeps falling and falling. The whole arrangement is designed for men who, at some time or other in their lives, were looking for something their own environment couldn't supply them with. Or they thought their own environment couldn't supply them with. So they gave up looking. They gave it up before they ever really even got started."[1]

You might have heard that more mountain-climbing deaths occur on the descent, not the ascent. On the way down, you're sore, worn out, and less focused. So you get sloppy. When inertia sends you sliding down the mountain you've worked so hard to climb up, you have to learn how to self-arrest. Jam that ice axe into the frozen ground and stop yourself from falling farther. The team you're roped up with can also stop your fall, but you're the one who has to take immediate action. Conversely, others on your team can also cause you to fall or you have to stop them from plummeting. As with mountaineering, in our daily lives it is critical to know the right techniques to self-arrest before you need them.

The friendly aspect of inertia helps create the velocity needed in your own personal rocket ship. Positive change and inertia are additive and addictive, kind of like booster rockets that keep propelling you to new heights. When you leave the atmosphere of your comfortable existence, it doesn't mean all is safe and satisfying. You will have to return to earth someday, in some way—gravity naturally will bring you down. It means sometimes you will return to visit friends and family who were not on your rocket journey of pursuing your passion. You'll find that you have changed, but they have not. It is kind of like being an expat and returning to your hometown with all of your amazing experiences and a radically altered worldview. In some cases, the friends and family you left behind appear as if their lives have stood still.

But just because your view has changed does not mean their lives have not.

Once you start rocketing onward in your spacecraft, you cannot necessarily turn the ship around. You can, however, make course corrections in direction and speed—these variables are under your control. One mistake is to look out your windows and judge yourself on how fast others are moving. Your flight plan is your flight plan, and others have their own. Unless they are direct competitors to you, which is rarely the case, you have to "stay the course."

For me, I don't deliver the longest drives on the golf course, but my drives are usually straight and most times I play from the fairway. When I try to alter my swing to hit the ball farther to match my competition, I hit it dead right or left or hit a complete shank. Ironically, even if I were to revamp my swing, take lessons, practice each day, and sacrifice short-term returns, I could still miss the breakthrough of complete change. True breakthrough requires commitment, time, and a willingness to go backward and get worse, before the change takes place and becomes permanent muscle memory. The point is to play your game—live your life—on your terms. When you make a commitment to change, you might go backward as you go forward—evolving what is in your control and in your innate abilities. The Cherokee have a saying: "Pay attention to the whispers so you won't have to hear the screams." A big whisper is if your stomach hurts every day before you go to work—I've had that experience at a past company and in past relationships. The only way to make those whispers, screams, and stomachaches go away is to change your inertia.

7 —

Questions to Help You Climb Higher

- If you did nothing and stayed your current course, speed, and direction, where do you think you would be in your personal and professional life in two to three years? Be honest with yourself, looking at the question in a clinical way.

- Are there Sherpas—likeminded supporters—you can turn to as a guide or advocate? These are people who will tell you the truth and give you authentic feedback.

- Are you prepared to make minor or major course corrections as you change your inertia?

Strategies for Success

How do you control this inertia? Start here:

1. Plot your course carefully, with checkpoints and milestones based on reality with the art of the possible. Just as when you encounter traffic on the highway, using your GPS to find alternate routes is important to get you to your desired destination.

2. Bring a crew. You are the captain of the ship, but choose your crew carefully. You need those who share your values and dreams, but also those who will steer you away from the debris in your path.

3. Have a Plan B and a Plan C. It does not mean you pull the lever on your escape module too quickly, but you'll also need time to get the parachute open before you crash land.

CHAPTER 2

AN IRISHMAN IN THE JUNGLE

Aidan Grimes Found His Purpose in a Bold Leap and a Long Journey

There are many angles to choose from when telling the story of Aidan Grimes—and the forces and choices that have shaped his life.

An obvious place to begin is in Dublin, Ireland, in 1964, the place of his birth. From there, you might focus on his working-class upbringing in that embattled city. It was a time of acute economic and political stress, which presented unique challenges and opportunities to a curious young boy.

For several years in the 1980s, he played professional soccer, starting at age sixteen with the Blackpool Football Club across the Irish Sea in England. Throughout his childhood, he battled through undiagnosed Asperger's Syndrome, a developmental disorder that hampers a person's ability to socialize and communicate.

When Aidan was twenty-one his father died of a sudden heart attack, leaving the family without a chance to say goodbye. In truth, many important things were left unsaid. Then in 1987, Aidan made a fateful and gut-wrenching decision to leave Ireland for a fresh start on the far side of the world in Australia.

Three decades later, he is still there—and has become highly respected in the fields of coaching, sports psychology, and motivational speaking. As well, he is an unsurpassed leader of a grueling and infamous ninety-six kilometer trek through the mountainous jungle of Papua New Guinea.

Those are important details, to be sure. But to truly understand Aidan's story, you need to view it in a much larger context. You must start with a World War II history lesson and the story of the legendary Kokoda Track Campaign in Papua New Guinea. It's a tale of integrity, honor, sacrifice, and extreme endurance in the face of overwhelming odds— all the values that have fueled Aidan's extraordinary life and shaped his vision for the world.

A Line in the Jungle

In March 1942—just three months after the Japanese attack at Pearl Harbor—Imperial Japanese commanders had their sights set on Australia, a key strategic objective in the South Pacific. Having just accepted the largest surrender of

British forces in history at Singapore on February 15, they sensed an opportunity to press their advance to include the "land down under."

Even though Australian forces were poorly organized, inadequately equipped, and overextended due to deployments in the European Theater, the Japanese High Command concluded that a full-fledged invasion was beyond the current capability of its military. Instead, they adopted a different goal—the capture of Port Moresby on the southeastern coast of Papua New Guinea, just a few hundred miles across the Coral Sea from Australia.

From Port Moresby, they reasoned, they could strike at Australia's most populous coastal industrial cities: Melbourne, Sydney, and Brisbane. A presence in Port Moresby would also allow the Japanese to control key shipping lanes between the Pacific and Indian Oceans and cut off the Aussies from American supply ships. Finally, the move would lay the groundwork for a future invasion of Australia at a more opportune moment.

In short, if they could not occupy the country, they would at least isolate and harass her and bide their time.

The first Japanese attempt to capture Port Moresby by direct amphibious assault was turned back in May 1942 during the Battle of the Coral Sea. Then, in June, the Imperial Japanese Navy took heavy losses in the Battle of Midway, dramatically reducing their capacity for amphibious operations in the South Pacific. That's when they decided on a different pathway to their goal: They would land troops on the northern coast of Papua New Guinea and mount an assault of Port Moresby over land—on the single-file mountainous jungle trail known as the Kokoda Track.

Kokoda is a village situated in the coastal lowlands north of the Owens Stanley Range, roughly halfway across the southeastern finger of Papua New Guinea. The Kokoda Track traverses some of the most difficult and remote terrain in the world. Starting at just over eleven hundred feet in Kokoda, the track climbs to the dizzying height of 7,380 feet (2,249 meters) at Mount Bellamy—though the total elevation gain experienced by hikers across the rugged landscape is much greater.

The jungle there is dense and unforgiving, and is home to numerous tropical diseases such as malaria. The climate is hot, humid, and prone to torrential amounts of rain. In other words, this is among the least ideal places on earth for a modern mechanized military operation.

Had the Japanese undertaken the overland assault of Port Moresby in February 1942, they most likely would have succeeded, virtually unopposed. Instead, they delayed the operation until late July. In the interim, Supreme Allied Commander in the South Pacific General Douglas MacArthur foresaw the threat of strategic Japanese advancement in Papua New Guinea and ordered defensive actions.

A militia of around three hundred native troops with Australian officers called the Papuan Infantry Battalion was already deployed at Kokoda. Major General Basil Morris ordered the 39th Infantry Battalion, garrisoned at Port Moresby, to augment those forces. The hundred-strong B Company left for Kokoda on July 7. Collectively, these units were known by the code name "Maroubra Force." They had scarcely reached their objective when news arrived of a Japanese incursion on the northern coast at Buna, just sixty miles away. On July 23, 1942, the advancing Japanese force made first contact with the undertrained and ill-equipped Papuan Infantry Battalion.

What followed is an epic tale of bravery, endurance, sacrifice and "mateship." Over the next four months, the outmatched Australian soldiers—affectionately known as "diggers"—made the Japanese invaders pay dearly for every inch of ground they gained along the track. As momentary tactical advantage swung back and forth between the two opposing forces, strategic advancement steadily favored the Japanese, with the Australians eventually falling back to a place called Imita Ridge on September 17—within sight of Port Moresby.

15 —

By this time, the Japanese supply lines along the single-file track were stretched to their limits. More importantly, Imperial Japanese forces were simultaneously suffering heavy losses during the Allied invasion of Guadalcanal, in the nearby Solomon Islands. As a result, the Japanese campaign to take Port Moresby came to a halt, with commanders ordered to adopt a defensive posture.

They began to fall back in late September. Australian units pursued them relentlessly and, on November 2, recaptured Kokoda. The campaign had claimed 6,600 Japanese lives, compared to 625 Australians. Many more were wounded or fell sick due to tropical disease.

Through January 1943, Allied forces assaulted the Japanese beachheads in the notably fierce Battle of Buna-Gona. Japanese soldiers fought to the death in defense of their positions—and Allied losses exceeded the rate experienced at Guadalcanal.

This Thing Called "Mateship"

Today, Aidan Grimes is one of Australia's leading authorities on the Kokoda Track Campaign. But his point of view is not that of an academic historian, remaining at a distance and searching dusty libraries for clues to what really happened during those fateful months of battle. Over the past twenty-four years, Aidan has retraced the steps of those heroic diggers and ill-fated Japanese soldiers—many times over. Nine times a year, he leads diverse groups of westerners on an eleven-day trek the length of the ninety-six kilometer Kokoda Track. In fact, it's believed that, having logged over a hundred trips (and counting), Aidan has walked the Kokoda Track more times than any other westerner.

His purpose? In part, to keep the history of the heroic campaign alive. His treks are punctuated by periodic presentations in which Aidan evokes the names and faces of young diggers, the sounds of gunfire, and the smell of powder. He points out rusted equipment, abandoned in the jungle seventy-five years ago, that offers tangible testimony to the gut-wrenching sacrifices of ordinary young men in defense of their country.

"These kids had no training. They were just Australians off the street with a gung-ho attitude, and they didn't give up," says Aidan, admiringly. "The story's about being totally overwhelmed and outnumbered, with no training or supplies, and yet they still came through. At the heart of it is a thing called 'mateship.'"

Mateship is the Australian term for human relationships that go beyond ordinary social ties. It's about being able to count on people in your community—in your tribe—no matter what. It's a concept that resonates with Aidan, hearkening back to his boyhood on the streets of Dublin, where being Irish was more than a label—it was a badge of belonging.

Since learning the story of the Kokoda Track nearly a quarter-century ago, Aidan has sought out the surviving members of the Maroubra Force and has been named an honorary member of a number of the units that took part in the fighting, including the original Papua Infantry Battalion, made up of native militia.

17 —

In addition, through the years Aidan has befriended the indigenous people who live in the jungles along the track. As a sign of respect for his strength and courage, locals have given him the name "Uda Baroma," meaning Wild Boar.

But that's only half the story. Even more important to him than providing a living history lesson, Aidan has learned that the grueling physical, mental, and emotional challenge of completing the trip is good medicine for many of the ills suffered by members of modern society—himself included. His clients include top executives from global companies like Apple and Microsoft.

"On the Kokoda Track, hikers are faced with a massive physical challenge, which of course becomes a massive mental challenge," Aidan says. "What we see quite clearly is that people have mental 'viruses.' When people are stressed, when they are put in environments where they are insecure, these unhealthy thoughts and beliefs become visible for us to see and to possibly heal."

According to Aidan, what people most often lack on day one of the trek is a sense of purpose in life, a sense of belonging to something larger than themselves.

"What they are looking for is, 'Where do I fit in? Where is my place in the tribe?'" Aidan says. "What happens is you peel back the layers of the onion, all the layers of society. What that does is help to activate the survival instinct. It's black and white—you're either going to die or you're not. There's no point in pretending, no point in telling lies, because it's not going work. Up there, it's pure honesty."

That's what people get when they embark on the track—the rare opportunity for brutally frank self-appraisal. For many, that results in a complete overhaul and a whole new set of goals by the time they reach the end.

"I get a lot of people around fifty-five years of age," Aidan says. "At eighteen, they went straight from school into university on the promise that they would get a degree and make a bunch of money. Then they get the job, the car, the house, and the kids. Along the way they sell their souls to these companies. There comes a point in time when they start asking, 'What am I doing? Where do I fit in? What are my values? Who am I?'"

That's where Aidan and the Kokoda expedition become so valuable. "Come with me up into the jungle," he says, "and I'll give you an opportunity to reset the clock back to when you started."

But it's not just older people who have already achieved "success" in life who find the ability to realign their lives according to new priorities. Aidan is especially proud of results he sees among soldiers returning from tours of duty in Afghanistan or Iraq who suffer from psychological distress as a result of their experiences. He also works with at-risk youth, teaching them how to find their place in the world by discovering their purpose and becoming useful to their tribe.

Yet all of this begs the question that Aidan himself freely poses: "I'm an Irishman in the jungle. How did I get here?"

The answer takes us all the way back to Ireland.

Leaving a Dead-end Life

In all great journeys there is a pivotal moment, a point in time in which all that could follow—all the achievements, growth, and advancement—hangs in the balance.

"The moment that nearly capsized me in my journey was waking up one day in Dublin and saying, 'I've got to get out of here,'" Aidan recalls. "I was going nowhere. It was a dead-end life. It was the hardest decision I've ever made, because my father had just passed away and it meant leaving my mother."

The death of his father galvanized for Aidan the radical idea—at least among his peers—that there had to be more to life than what he could see around him in Ireland. In the 1980s, unemployment among men his age was more than 20 percent, and opportunities for overcoming that disadvantage were scarce.

"There was no way in the world we were ever going to go to university, and we knew that," Aidan recalls. "The best you could ever do would be to get a civil service job, if you were lucky, or become a tradesman."

Or, in his own case, to play soccer. At sixteen, he had signed a contract with the Blackpool Football Club in Blackpool, England. That foray into the world of professional sports was his first real wake-up call that his innate Irish optimism might not always be enough to get by on.

"Living in an occupied country taught us a sense of optimism," he says. "We learned to say that tomorrow can only get better. It had to get better, because it couldn't get any worse. But when I went to Blackpool, I realized there was an element I'd never seen before, and that was playing for money. That meant the other players would protect their position at all costs. To them, I was going over there to take their job. To me, soccer had always been how we communicated and related to each other as a tribe. Suddenly, I was in a professional setting, and they wouldn't even pass the ball to me."

Back in Dublin, after a stint with another team, he started to suspect that his future there was stunted. He saw men "sitting in the same seat at the pub, telling the same stories," year after year. And he knew that was not for him.

"I made a decision to go to Australia, purely a drive for something bigger, something better. For more. It became a rite of passage, where you're standing naked on top of the hill, and it's all up to you. You've really got to walk the talk."

It was a costly decision, however. It meant leaving behind the only tribe he'd ever known, with no guarantee he'd find another to replace it. His identity was rooted in the music, stories and history of Ireland, particularly in the solidarity of resistance to British rule. But worst of all, his desire for a new start meant saying goodbye to his mother just a few months after his father died.

"But I knew that my dreams had gotten bigger than anything I could see around me," he says. "I had outgrown Ireland."

Aidan bought a ticket and, with $2,000 in his pocket, he set out for the land down under. He arrived in Sydney on October 3, 1987, and made his way to Pitch Street—on the very day of a large parade to honor soldiers who had served Australia in the Vietnam War and others. He watched as an old veteran struggled to keep up, but refused the help of his "mates," determined to walk on his own.

"I stood watching with tears in my eyes. It was a major moment of learning in my life," Aidan recalls. "In Ireland, we know our culture and where we belong. Most importantly, we know where we're going because of our history. I made a promise that day that I'd get to know this new country, Australia. I vowed to get to know its culture and its heartbeat."

It was a serendipitous beginning that instilled in him a desire to know the history of his new home, to learn of its heroes and their sacrifices, much as he knew the stories of his own past in Ireland. It was the very desire that would eventually lead him to the jungles of Papua New Guinea and his passion for retelling what happened there.

To keep that promise, however, he'd have to live through some frightening moments: down to his last dollar, making a single fish from the market last for days; being unable to find work without "telling a few lies"; and the loneliness of being half a world away from home—until he found a new tribe in Australia.

"From where I'm sitting now, I know that the journey I've led people on in the jungle has been my own journey," he says. "All these years, I've been the one in search of a tribe. How does an Irishman from the streets of Dublin end up in Papua New Guinea lecturing Australians on their history? All those things were about my search. I've dragged people along on that journey and been able to pass along some of what I've learned."

What he's learned, he sums up in a riddle: "How do you eat an elephant? One bite at a time." How do you endure the Kokoda Track in tropical heat? By placing one foot in front of the other.

And how do you break free of inertia and create the life you want? Don't be afraid to stand naked on a hill—like an Irishman in the jungle

CHAPTER 3

THE SIGNPOST SAYS, "TURN HERE"

Watch for the Signals That Tell You It's Time to Leap

"Ignoring the signs is a good way to end up at the wrong destination."
Unknown

Y ou know you're ready for a big leap forward in your life when you recognize a sign, be it a tiny ember glowing in your heart or a bolt of lightning that strikes you on the head.

The sign may come from someplace unexpected—a song, a movie, a Facebook post, or a conversation. It also could have been building in your mind. It might come from a fight with your spouse, a work restructuring, a catastrophe, or a health scare. An experience brings something up in your lizard brain, or maybe it's an issue you've been thinking about for a long while. Or maybe it's something you did as a kid, like suffering through piano lessons—but now you suddenly want to learn how to play pop songs on your keyboard. At the extreme, you watched a program on illiteracy in Africa and decided to join an NGO in Tanzania.

David Whyte writes in *Crossing the Unknown Sea—Work as a Pilgrimage of Identity*, "Every person comes to a place, at one time or another in their maturation, of complete loss and deadness, a stark and frightening absence of creativity and enthusiasm."[1] You might see these signs of impending change when you are in that state of loss and deadness.

Signs can come from everywhere—visual, electronic, audible, or a dream while sleeping. Listen to yourself when you are telling your close friend or Sherpa about it. Are you excited but scared, motivated but daunted? Are you describing something that is more of a fantasy, like playing center for an NBA basketball team? Or are you looking at a new job and know deep down that despite early enthusiasm, you would pretty quickly get restless and want to move on again?

Shannon Adler, in her book *300 Questions to Ask Your Parents Before It's Too Late*, writes:

> We often look outwardly for signs and divine guidance to navigate the choices we must make in life. But what if the signs we seek were more internal? Maybe our answer has always been found

in our true feelings—the ones that were not guided by circumstances, timing or obstacles . . . the dreams we wanted as a child. Maybe, we are not confused at all. . . . Maybe we were looking for the miracle to avoid the hard work it would take to achieve it. Therefore, the miracles we sit here waiting for are not to be seen with the eyes, but felt in our heart. Maybe the miracle we have prayed for was always inside of us—the gift to live how we truly feel.[2]

There are indeed not many miracles in our lives unless you win the lottery. Even then, you have to play to win. In the same vein, you have to put yourself out there and open your heart and soul to your own potential.

A sign of change or new direction does not have to have a direct impact on just one thing in your life. For instance, you could decide to be a better father and husband by taking a new job or starting a new business that allows you to be home more. You could decide to lose weight and run a marathon because you saw a poster.

Look and Learn

In 2001, David Batstone discovered that his favorite Bay Area restaurant had been the center of a local human trafficking ring that forcibly brought hundreds of teenagers from India into the United States. He realized this was part of a rapidly expanding issue affecting every industry and area of the earth.

From there, Batstone wrote the book *Not For Sale* in 2007, and his non-profit organization was born. In the years since then, Not For Sale has worked with thousands of young people around the world, protecting them from human trafficking and modern-day slavery.

Batstone's amazing work began because his eyes were opened to problems and possibilities. This ability to perceive and receive is often the beginning of a big life change. Most every person I've ever met in marathons, mountain climbing, extreme sports, or philanthropy can articulate in great detail the moment, the place, the spark, and the decision that led them to pursue their passion. The signal was not seen in blinking neon lights, but there were signs that directed them to make a change.

You can get the same description from every wife who finally decided to leave her abusive, alcoholic husband. Or every unhappy worker who finally said to his terrible boss, "Take this job and shove it." There was a final, decisive moment—but they listened and acted on the signs they had seen for some time along the way.

I know these signposts. I saw one hanging from a streetlight in Stockholm on a cold, dark winter night and signed up for my first marathon. I saw another when a friend gave me the book *Into Thin Air* and, unlike millions who had read it, decided to climb the seven summits.

We are all aware of extreme signs, such as the one seen by Richard Dreyfus in the movie *Close Encounters of the Third Kind*. In the film, Dreyfus becomes obsessed with a mountain-like shape and starts making endless models of it. His obsession nearly destroys his sanity, life, and marriage in the process. Of course, it's a movie with a happy ending. I follow people on Facebook who are obsessed with animal rights and the humane treatment of all animals. I believe in this cause as well, but we must ask what we are doing about it, rather than just making and sharing more posts.

In the riveting movie *Tim's Vermeer*, main character Tim Jenison is obsessed with trying to duplicate the work of Johannes Vermeer and his famous painting, "The Music Lesson." On one hand, you have to hand it to Tim for using all of his inventive, scientific, and artistic skills. On the other hand, it's hard to imagine going through all he does for the reasons he does it. (See the movie and judge for yourself.) The point is, there's a difference between commitment and obsession. Though they both might ultimately accomplish the same goal, embarking on a career change, moving cross-country, or joining a cause has to involve a balanced approach.

So, in the end, your passion or goal might be what you do, but it will never define who you are. Yes, I summited Everest and the seven summits and completed marathons on seven continents, but those accomplishments definitely do not comprise who I am, nor what I want to define me.

You're Not Just What You Do

When you are at a party and someone asks you what you do for a living, how do you respond? You might say, "I'm senior director of strategic planning at Widgets Incorporated." Or, "I'm a stay-at-home mom of five kids." But there has to be a better answer. Someone told me about author Robert Fulghum and how he answers the question, "So what do you do?" He used to make up stories—telling people he was a neurosurgeon, janitor, or priest.

Later he created a business card that just read "Fulghum." This to him meant son, father, husband, friend, singer, dancer, eater, breather, sleeper, janitor, dishwasher, and so on. He doesn't want to be defined—or labelled—by just one title or phrase. There's a great quote Fulghum uses to describe himself: "I and you—we are infinite, rich, large, and contradictory, living, breathing, miracles—free human beings, children of God and the everlasting universe. That's what we do." Well said, right?

Words are powerful, and how we describe ourselves and how we think of ourselves matters. When you see the signposts and feel yourself called to your passions with purpose, think about your core competencies—what you are really good at. Then think about those things that you are really and truly passionate about. Now make a little diagram of these two areas and look for the intersection of innate skills and passions to help you decide where to go in your rocketship journey.

Later, we'll explore how to start the process of following your passions, including the expected obstacles and the potential pain and setbacks. We will also examine how to enlist support from your friends and family to form your own personal Sherpa crew. What you decide to do after this does not have to be the biggest and baddest thing ever attempted (but it could).

You'll need a stable base (stability) in order to act with a sense of speed to create your own agility brand (stability

+ speed = agility). You'll learn to create your own mission, vision, and SMART (Strategic, Measurable, Achievable, Realistic, and Time-bound) goals just like any good business.

Entrepreneur and business celebrity Mark Cuban once famously said, "Don't follow your passion—follow your effort." I would amend Cuban's quote to say, "Follow your energy to follow your passion."

Some words of caution as you are reading the signs and tea leaves: Make sure you don't damage your relationships with your family or friends in the process. In 1972, Apollo astronaut Eugene Cernan was the last man to walk on the moon, leaving his footprints and his daughter's initials in the dust. In the 2014 movie *Last Man on the Moon*, Cernan acknowledged that he was not present and available for his wife for the years of training during his Gemini and Apollo missions. Later, he was so busy with celebrity appearances and other activities that he ended up getting divorced from the wife who had stood by him.

29 —

He eventually remarried and has been married to his second wife for almost twenty-five years. Interestingly, in the movie as he travels from place to place giving inspirational speeches and book signings, he candidly talks about being gone from his wife for long periods, and you wonder whether he is making the same mistakes again.

The other big question you need to ask yourself is whether you'd really and truly be happy doing that thing you're passionate about. If you want to go and work in Africa for that NGO, could you really endure living in a tent with no running water or toilets when you've been used to a First-World lifestyle your entire life?

You can, however, "try on" your passion just as you would with a coat before you buy it. Volunteer for a two-week trip with your non-profit of choice; see if the process still stirs your blood once you "try it on." The signs will lead you to start your journey, but they won't warn you about what to expect during the hard times.

Questions to Help You Climb Higher

1. If you could do anything other than what you're doing now, what would it be? This is not like a bucket-list item you check off for a place you went or something you did. Think big about your life, career, and activities.

2. Then ask the why question: Why do you want to pursue this particular passion?

3. Who else will this benefit, and how will this endeavor or passion contribute to how you'll be remembered—your legacy? What causes do you believe in? Can you change yourself and also help be a part of changing the world? Can you truly be selfless at times?

Strategies for Success

How do you look for and react to the signposts pointing toward a meaningful change in your life? Here are some suggestions:

1. Don't ignore an idea in your head that won't go away. It keeps surfacing for a reason.

2. Try to quantify how much you feel inspired versus uninspired. When you feel uninspired 51 percent of the time, month after month, it's a signal that you're ready for your next big adventure.

3. Be aware of your emotions and energy when you start the day. It's a sure sign if you get out of bed in the morning dreading what's ahead rather than motivated by it.

4. Look for and be receptive to these signs. Open your heart to the universe with love, goodness and gratitude.

5. Tear down the signs in your head that say, *You can't do this.* Just imagine you have the fictional Stuart Smalley in your head saying, "I'm good enough, I'm smart enough, and doggone it, people like me!" And laugh about it.

CHAPTER 4

SHE FOUND HER VOICE

Once Stifled and Suppressed, Susan Overland Finally Said Yes to Her Real Self

Susan Freeman looked through the windshield of her "crappy brown Datsun" at the steady rain that had brought rush hour traffic to a standstill on a darkening fall evening in Santa Clara, California. The bleak, gray world of metal and concrete she saw outside was the mirror image of what she felt on the inside.

The car resembled her life as well—full of things that no longer worked: no heater, no air conditioner, and no radio. Black smoke belched from the tailpipe—a grievous social and environmental offense in the mid-90s in the Golden State. Worst of all, the driver's side window refused to roll up more than halfway, so the rain that evening felt highly personal, as if it fell just for her—a cold, soaking reminder that she would never have a right to expect more from life than this.

It was an apt culmination—in a twisted sort of way—to a recent avalanche of painful events in her life. Sitting in the rain, trying to keep her cigarette dry, Susan relived in her mind a series of phone conversations she'd had over the past twenty-four hours, starting with the private high school her sons attended:

"Mrs. Freeman?"

"Yes."

"This is the finance office at Bellarmine High School. I'm sorry to have to make this call, but your son's tuition is overdue and if we don't receive the payment soon, he will not be able to graduate with his class."

Next in line was the bank:

"Mrs. Freeman?"

"Yes."

"We've had to return three of your checks this week and your overdraft charges may make it necessary for us to close your checking account if the monies are not deposited this week."

To make matters much worse, the phone rang again:

"Mrs. Freeman?"

"Yes."

"I'm calling from the payroll department at Santa Clara University to notify you that we've received a levy against your wages from the Franchise Tax Board [the California version of the IRS]."

"How much will they take from my salary?"

"Well, they can take from 50 to 70 percent, unless you can get them to make other arrangements."

But most devastating of all:

"Mrs. Freeman, this is Officer Smith from the fraud division of San Jose Police Department. Is your husband Al Freeman?"

"Yes, why?"

"He was arrested today on embezzlement charges. He's given us a statement that clears your name, but we need you to voluntarily come in for questioning, or we'll have to send an officer to pick you up. When can you come in?"

"Oh, how I hated 'Mrs. Freeman,'" Susan says, recalling that evening years later. "The more I replayed those conversations, the more I began to contemplate how I might put an end to it all. Could I make my death look like an accident? Surely the boys would be fine—my sister would make sure they never wanted for anything. Really, wouldn't they be better off without me? Where the hell is God, anyway, and why won't He give me some sign if I should go on living?"

***

When Susan was a young girl, there were no visible clues that her life journey would lead to such a dark place—stuck in the grip of hopelessness and despair. In spite of growing up with parents who struggled with alcoholism and abusiveness, as early as age seven she recalls feeling an "amazing spiritual connection" to God when sitting in mass at the Catholic church her family attended.

"It was usually when people started talking that I lost the connection," she quips. "I was the kid in class at Catholic school who always raised my hand to ask the weird questions, like, 'How come my friends who don't go to Catholic school aren't gonna go to heaven?' and 'what do you mean they're gonna go to hell?' None of it made sense."

Music and theater were central to her life as a young person. She sang and performed every chance she got—in school plays and other events, even lying about her age in order to work as an entertainer in Manhattan supper clubs. She loved it and dreamed of one day making a career for herself in music theater.

All that changed abruptly when Susan met her first husband and eloped with him to Las Vegas. Within three months, she was pregnant with her first child. A baby boy was born before her twenty-first birthday.

"I didn't even have a driver's license, but I had a kid," she says.

Though she didn't know it at the time, Susan had begun the process of losing her voice—not literally, but in the way that so many people do when their boundaries are compromised and dreams thwarted. Over the next twenty years, her ability to speak for herself slowly atrophied, taking with it the belief that she even had a right to do so. Along the way, the light of her innate curiosity and natural spiritual connection with God slowly went out as well. The shining life she had dreamed of faded into one long struggle with financial and emotional hardship.

"I came to the place where I believed I was living the life I deserved," Susan recalls. "I told myself, 'this is all I'm gonna get.'"

***

Traffic showed no sign of moving yet on the streets of Santa Clara that evening, and the rain continued to fall. The question on Susan's mind just kept getting heavier: "Where is God, anyway?"

Suddenly, she saw a beautiful woman in her mirror, standing in the rain behind her car. She appeared to be perfect—everything Susan felt she was not. An angel, perhaps?

"She was tall and thin, while I was the fattest I had ever been in my life," Susan remembers. "While I was dressed for neglect, she was dressed for success, pencil thin in her designer high heels, perfectly tailored black suit, white blouse, and matching designer bag dangling off her wrist. She had long, beautifully highlighted hair—mine was short and prematurely gray, with a bad $5 haircut."

Susan wondered if it was a vision meant to show her what could have been. What might still be? Then she noticed that the driver's side door of the shiny BMW ahead of the Datsun stood open. Somehow the woman had walked by unnoticed. Looking again, Susan saw that she held a small spiral notebook and pencil, hurriedly writing something down. She got out of the car and joined the "angelic vision" on the road.

"Excuse me, what are you doing?" she asked.

"Writing down your license plate number."

"What? What for?"

"Because you are polluting the air, and I'm going to report you."

"You need to get in your car, right now," Susan told the woman, barely containing her anger. "Get in your car right now before I kill you!"

The woman could see Susan's state of mind and quickly returned to her car. Susan got back in hers as well, and set about trying to light a fresh cigarette with trembling hands. Just then the driver in the car behind her honked his horn—even though traffic was still frozen in place and there was clearly nowhere for Susan to go.

"I didn't honk back," she says. "Instead, I stuck my arm out my half-open window and raised my middle finger as high as it would go. And then I laughed. Well, actually, 'laughed' is not quite the right word. I howled, guffawed—a boisterous, from-the-gut laugh that left tears streaming down my face. I hadn't felt this good in a long time."

***

Making threats and flipping people off in traffic are not normally seen as evidence of a spiritual awakening. Yet, for Susan, that's exactly what her life-changing experience in a rain-soaked traffic jam became. That "middle finger" was aimed far more at her own limiting beliefs, and the dark status quo she'd been living, than at another person. What she was tempted to "kill" in that moment was the woman she had become—a depleted shell of herself who believed she deserved to be mistreated and downtrodden.

Her outrage marked a pivotal moment in her life—the moment she said "yes" to a different future.

"I asked God for a sign as to why I should keep on living, and there she was, a self-appointed smog reporter who looked like a supermodel," Susan says. "In that instant I heard God say, 'You should keep on living, Susan, because you're a good person, and I need you. I need you to yank your thoughts out of this slum and remember who you are! And more importantly, I need you to remember who I am, and then go teach others!'"

Over the next several years, that's exactly what she did.

First, she made contact with everyone who'd phoned her with bad news during the previous day. In each case, she worked out a deal that forestalled disaster and allowed her to slowly dig out of her financial hole.

Second, she left a job she hated in a "toxic, dysfunctional work environment" and took a new one that eventually led to a position as executive assistant to a senior vice president at

Hewlett-Packard. There she worked her way up to a six-figure compensation package and the respect of her colleagues. She started seeing a counselor who helped her recognize how she'd lost her voice—and offered sound advice about how to get it back.

"My therapist once said, 'You keep talking about how your husband wanted things in life, and your mom, and many others—but you still haven't said what you want.' I burst into tears, partly because nobody had ever asked me that before, and also because I wasn't sure I knew how to answer her."

The counselor gently suggested that reclaiming her lost love for music and theater might be a good place to start. Shortly after that, a small, square ad in the newspaper caught her eye—announcing auditions for an upcoming production at the Sunnyvale Community Players. She got a part. She hired a voice coach and soon was back on stage as often as she could manage it.

Susan divorced her husband and several years later married someone new. Max Overland was a kindred spirit who shared her renewed interest in finding a healthy faith community that would help anchor their new life. That led them to the Center for Spiritual Living in San José—a vibrant church with a bold mission:

> We believe that life is good, that God is all there is, and that love is the only power. We are a welcoming and inclusive community of inspired individuals caring for and about each other and the entire planetary family, bringing the gifts of active compassion and kindness to the world. Our purpose

is to transform lives, build dreams, and reveal God through education, music, prayer, service, generosity, and play.

After feeling unworthy, alone, and abandoned by God for nearly two decades, the possibility of such free and affirming reconnection to spiritual purpose called to her deeply. She began a new journey, first as a licensed "Prayer Practitioner" in the church and then—after three years of intensive study to earn a master's degree in Consciousness Studies—as a full-time minister since 2011.

***

For a while, Susan Overland lost her voice—and herself. She got it all back, and more, when she said "Yes!" to a different way of seeing herself and God.

"I now know that I was settling for a known hell rather than what could be a potential paradise," she says. "There was always a boogie man in the closet that I kept giving my power to. The biggest thing was to actually believe the spiritual principle that there is a power for good in the universe and that we can use it. But even more importantly, it can use us—if we just say yes and stop giving in to fear."

CHAPTER 5

RESISTANCE IS FUTILE

Recognize What's Holding You Back
and Push It Out of the Way

"To fly, we have to have resistance."
Maya Lin

Webster's Dictionary defines resistance as "the refusal to accept or comply with something; the attempt to prevent something by action or argument." With this definition as our springboard, let's explore what's holding you back—those challenges from within—after you've seen the signs and decided to make a change in your direction and inertia.

Almost all of us struggle with a fear of failure—and for many of us, an equal fear of success, which might cause us to self-sabotage. We can understand the fear of failure, but why do many of us have a fear of success?

The reasons are many, of course, but one of them is simply that with success comes higher expectations. Think about the breakthrough singer whose first album reaches number one on the charts, followed by the talk show circuit and glossy magazine spreads. The hardest part now is to channel her energy into a second, even better, album now that a big fan base eagerly awaits the new release. This is why we have so many one-hit wonders: They fail to reach the heights again after initial success.

Another example is in sports, where the "sophomore curse" is a mainstream saying. You see this in college football or major league baseball. The first season, a player is a freshman phenom—catches are made, touchdowns are scored, and the team becomes a top-ten contender. Or a rookie pitcher amasses strikeouts, maintains a low earned-run average, and helps his team make the playoffs.

Oftentimes in the second season the other teams have figured out the player's strategy and weaknesses. Opponents have watched film and know how to play defense against him, or how to wait on the fastball or hit his curve.

Also, the player has experienced fame and fortune, and her time is diverted and focus distracted. She does interviews, cultivates a social media presence, and makes appearances instead of practicing, training and honing her craft.

She could also, somewhere inside, feel she is not worthy of the adoration and, as a result, actively self-sabotages.

How many athletes have we seen self-destruct after they've become successful? Too many to count.

As we prepare to use resistance and overcome our fears, we have to be equally prepared for the success we're envisioning. How can we keep the momentum going and manage potential "fame and fortune"—even if it's on a much smaller scale than rock stars or sports heroes? Those who stay grounded in their family and their team, and who "up their game" through focused training, are the ones who have multi-year success rates. Good examples are actors like Tom Hanks and Ron Howard, who by all accounts are genuinely nice guys in solid marriages with careers that have evolved to see them become major directors and producers.

There are many fine examples of those who hone their craft over many decades but remain humble, good human beings over time. One who comes to mind is the great Los Angeles Dodgers broadcaster Vin Scully. He started broadcasting for the Brooklyn Dodgers in 1950 and retired at the end of the 2016 season after sixty-seven years—yes, sixty-seven years!

In his final home game broadcasting for the team, with the fans waving "Win for Vin" signs, the Dodgers hit a walk-off homerun with two outs in the tenth inning to secure the win for Vin. During a post-game ceremony with fifty thousand fans cheering and his wife of forty-three years by his side, Vin's opening line to the stadium was, "Aw, c'mon, it's just me." What a role model for all of us—Vin was success

45 —

personified, humility displayed, and grace shown . . . not occasionally, but always.

Move Forward in the Face of Fear

Mark Twain said, "Courage is resistance to fear, mastery of fear, not absence of fear." Besides the fear of success, the main resistance comes from fear of failure. We live in a society fixated on instant gratification, and we're told we can "get rich quick" and "lose twenty pounds in one week." We hear about "overnight stars" and people achieving their "fifteen minutes of fame." We don't even like waiting five minutes for our double mocha skinny lattés at Starbucks.

We want everything and we want it now. We hate the saying, "Good things happen to those who wait." We'd rather say, "Good people don't wait for things to happen."

We also want guarantees, and we want guaranteed happiness. Benjamin Franklin said, "In this world, nothing can be said to be certain except death and taxes." True, there aren't many guarantees in life—and certainly not happiness.

Why do we have so much resistance to change when we want to pursue our higher purpose? Grab a hold of these words by automobile pioneer Henry Ford, who said, "When everything seems to be going against you, remember that the airplane takes off against the wind, not with it."

Some potential obstacles to change include:

- **Finances.** We fear losing our savings or not being able to put food on the table for our family.

- **Peer groups or pressure**. You might fear becoming an object of ridicule, with friends saying, "Why is she trying to do this? She'll never make it!"

- **Society**. Our culture as a whole tends to want to keep us in our norms, categories, and roles—there is societal resistance to change.

- **Jealousy and animosity**. Others may grow jealous or resentful because you had the courage to step out. There will always be haters who really don't want to see you happy. They'll say things like, "He used to be our friend. Now he thinks he's a big shot."

- **Being labelled as crazy**. People will think you've lost your mind or are living in some sort of fantasy world. They'll say things to you (or about you behind your back) like, "She's moving overseas? She won't last a month!" Or, "He has no experience starting a business. How can he possibly think this is going to work?"

- **Resistance to leaving our comfort zone**. If we leave our current job, we're fearful of losing our administrative support, our embedded colleagues and built-in subordinates, the structure, regular pay checks, and restricted stock units.

- **Criticism of your happiness.** People might say things like, "No one can be that happy." Some friends might see you in a loving and intimate relationship and root for drama and hardship. It's why people love gossip rags—some people just don't want to read a story

47 —

about Jennifer Aniston celebrating another happy wedding anniversary.

- **Loss of friends.** By moving in a new direction, you run the risk of placing yourself outside your circle of friends. When you decide to make a change—give up drinking, go back to school, become a vegetarian—some of your friends will give you grief and apply peer pressure. They'll say, "Come party with us—you can always study tomorrow." Or, "C'mon, just one drink—what's it going to hurt?" Since they might have trouble sticking to their own convictions and commitments, they don't like it when you stick to yours. They might wish they had the courage to do what you're doing.

- **Lack of support or encouragement from your spouse or significant other.** An unsupportive spouse or partner can cause relational friction, which can come from the other person being competitive, insecure, or fearful of financial instability. I love the classic scene in the film *Parenthood* when Steve Martin's character quits his job and comes home to tell his wife, Karen (Mary Steenburgen). She tells him she's pregnant and adds, "Maybe this isn't the best time to quit your job."

- **Your partner's fear of your change.** Your partner might also fear that you will change after you've achieved your goal—that person doesn't want you to turn into a workaholic, control freak, tightwad, or egomaniac. Your life change, especially if it is a major one, will almost certainly affect your relationship. But the relationship shift will likely be for the positive, because you will be feeling more energized and passionate.

The Problem with Perfection

One of the biggest obstacles to change comes from waiting for the perfect time or the perfect plan—which might never come. It's possible to do *too much* research and spend too much time on Google, Facebook, or LinkedIn. It's the "paralysis of analysis" that stops many of us.

You have to know that resistance is futile, despite all the resistance you're going to run into—finances, relationships, fears, society. As you prepare for your leap forward, your heart and soul will be continually pulled into your passion like a celestial body being pulled toward a shining sun.

If this thing you want to do is truly your passion, your body will have a constant itch that needs to be scratched. All the green-light signs will keep popping up and will reinforce what you already know. Resistance is indeed futile. Inertia will keep raising its ugly head, and though you might continue to resist, eventually the passion will take over completely. You will feel compelled, even duty-bound, to pursue what you want to do.

Think about the largely unknown backstory of actor Kris Kristofferson. At an early age, he was an aspiring songwriter. That was his passion. He won a Rhodes scholarship to Oxford University, and then joined the Army, attending Ranger school. He was a boxer and later became a captain in the Army in Germany, before becoming a helicopter pilot. As if all this was not enough, he went on to teach English literature at West Point.

Despite all of these achievements and the ability to excel in any number of fields, a passion gripped his heart and wouldn't let go. He eventually knew resistance was futile, so he moved to Nashville and ended up sweeping floors at a music studio. His parents and grandparents, with their own military careers, disowned him. With his own determination, he became the famous singer and actor we've known for the past several decades—and who is still singing and performing as this is written at age eighty.

I also think about the story of my climbing friend Paula, who had to turn around above twenty-eight thousand feet on Mt. Everest. Paula was forced to concede due to disastrous avalanches and earthquakes and was unable to summit with everyone else in her group. Five years after her first attempt, in May 2016, she stood atop Mt. Everest on her fourth expedition, never doubting her conviction.

Paula's passion overcame all the opposition the mountain and circumstances had thrown at her. She faced resistance from finances, friends, and the fear of having to turn back yet again. Some people had told her, "Honey, you almost made it to the top, and you've been higher than most everyone in the world. Why not give up and be happy with what you have?" She didn't listen to the naysayers, and I'm so glad she pressed on. I can only imagine the self-satisfaction she gained by summiting and returning safely.

So what can we do once we understand that this resistance is, in fact, futile? Shift your perspective to view resistance as a positive force and not a negative force. You need resistance to bring out your best. Think about weight training at the gym. Without resistance, you would have nothing to test and would be unable to build your strength. The resistance you leverage physically in the gym and the mental resistance you fight in life can only build strong character.

Consider also that we would never fly in an airplane or our rocket ship without air resistance. According to Universetoday. com, "Air resistance describes the forces that are in opposition to the relative motion of an object as it passes through the air. These drag forces act opposite to the oncoming flow velocity, thus slowing the object down. . . . Air resistance is the result of collisions of the object's leading surface with air molecules."

Resistance is indeed the force that builds our muscles and the wind beneath our wings. When you're ready for the next big step in your life, expect resistance and embrace resistance. Use it to get stronger and fly higher.

Questions to Help You Climb Higher

1. *What* is your resistance? Why does it exist? How much of this "pushback" is mental versus other more natural factors (physical, family, financial)?

2. *How* can you best utilize this resistance to give you the courage to overcome your fears? How can you leverage resistance to lift off like a plane using the physics and embodiment of your dream?

3. *Who* do you need to lean on to help you overcome resistance? Identify those awesome cheerleaders who will say, "You were totally meant to do this. Don't give up!"

Strategies for Success

How then do we make this resistance and drag work for us? Some tips:

1. Honor and acknowledge your dream and passion. Empower it, giving it life and meaning. Accept your dream and embrace your passion.

2. Both accept and accelerate the timing of your dream and passion. Maybe you can't make the leap right now, but there are many things you can do to prepare. In addition to online research, seek out and talk to those in the field you want to be in. Ask what they did and how they really got there—but resist the temptation to compare. Prepare your business plan. Pursue an intermediate mountain—something, anything, to keep the pot simmering. This middle step will help you to put on the afterburners at the appropriate time.

3. Build and rely on your network of supporters, friends and family. They will also test your resistance, seeing how committed you really are and checking your resolve. You'll work through some tough conversations and experience how to build your muscle mass for when it is time to strike.

Just as in fitness training, there will be initial soreness, both mental and physical. You'll constantly think, *I can't do this anymore.* In resistance training, you become stronger each and every time you exercise those muscles and use resistance to your advantage. You will begin to crave the next challenge just as a bodybuilder hungers for the next workout. Resistance is futile but not impossible. Remember that you want to have no regrets when it's your time to leave this planet. People always say they wish they had done something big while they still could. You won't be one of those. You will make the leap.

CHAPTER 6

MUSIC, MAGIC, AND
THE MEANING OF LIFE

Leaving Behind Fame and Acclaim, Miha Pogacnik
Now Helps Transform the World Through Art

Violinist Miha Pogacnik is a modern-day wizard.

True, in recent decades, words like that have lost their meaning through misuse and marketing hyperbole. When anyone with something to sell can force powerful language to serve small and ignoble goals, it's easy to forget that such things as genuine wizardry and magic still exist.

Occasionally, however, a person comes along to remind us, and Miha is one of them. Born in 1949 in war-ravaged Slovenia, he is a true master of musical magic—not content simply to entertain or enthrall an audience, or to bask in praise and applause.

As a young man, Miha achieved all of that, ascending to the top among his peers to become a rising-star soloist, sought after and respected. His path into "greatness" was laid out before him, and traditional "success" was his for the taking. Instead, he walked away and chose a different road. Or, to be precise, he carved his own, brand-new course through the wilderness of limited and limiting options.

"Something was fundamentally wrong—that you put so much energy into mastering your skills and the magic, and then when you are finished people applaud and they love it, and then it's over," Miha says, his words shaped by an endearing Slovenian accent. "They go home to drink or sit in front of the television. I always felt that when the concert is finished, then the beginning should happen, not the end."

Since leaving a conventional life behind, he has pursued that elusive "beginning" across a long and winding career, marked by bold action and visionary thinking. The years have forged him, turning him into an alchemist bent on harnessing the mystical power of music to turn the base metals of the present-day human condition into the original, magical gold we all possess, but have forgotten lies within us. It's a grand mission aimed at nothing short of the social and cultural transformation of the world.

"In the deepest province of the human soul, there is magic," he says. "That's what we are. Unfortunately, there is so much dust and ash covering it these days. In essence what I do is go around opening the dampers in people's lives so the fire flares up again."

Taming Turbo Capitalism

To grasp the nature of Miha's twenty-first-century work— what he refers to as his "fourth life"—imagine yourself in his "laboratory." Picture a broad stage where all the skilled musicians in a philharmonic orchestra are seated in curved rows, instruments at the ready, eyes on their conductor. Feel the breathless anticipation in the sudden silence as Miha lifts his violin bow, all the potential energy of a musical masterpiece awaiting release. The music begins, and a galaxy of dancing sound appears in the room.

57 —

Yet in this scene you don't play the role of detached observer looking down from the balcony. You are embedded in it, seated in a row of chairs placed between the stringed instruments and the woodwinds. You feel the vibrating frequencies of music caress your skin through the air and rumble in your bones as it rises out of the floor. Your heart expands with emotion until you fear you'll burst. The music is a buoyant force that nearly lifts you free of gravity itself.

The picture isn't complete, however, until you look to your left and right and see the true purpose behind the gathering of musicians. Without this, the entire exercise is just another performance of timeless music—marvelous, perhaps, but without the full potential for the kind of alchemy Miha seeks to create.

Because seated beside you are a number of high-ranking executives from some of the world's largest and wealthiest corporations. These are powerful men and women, decision-makers, whose actions every day have profound influence over the lives of millions of others—trillions, if you include the non-human creatures with whom we share the planet. They sit in boardrooms and back rooms around the world and literally chart the future of humankind through the values they express in their choices and priorities.

"Some start crying," Miha muses. "It's like a catharsis. They remember they are human. They forget their power and rank. If you get people close to that point, then suddenly everything is possible, and it's not just the bottom line and profit margins. The real things come to the surface."

Miha believes society has lost sight of a fundamental truth: the world's economy must exist to serve the needs of the people, not the other way around. His remedy is to confront the "anomaly of one-sided economic thinking" with an alternative way of seeing, found in the power of great art to restore equilibrium. To do that, he goes straight to the top of the corporate chain of command.

A Backward Accordion

That sweeping vision has humble roots in the industrial city of Kranj, Slovenia. In 1952, Miha was three years old, in a nation still suffering in the aftermath of World War II and coming to grips with the new reality of belonging to the post-war Soviet Bloc. Modern entertainments like television were non-existent, but each weekend the family would walk for the better part of a day into the mountains for traditional celebrations of music and food.

"I became amazed at how the people enjoyed the music, how they danced to the accordion," Miha recalls. "When my father saw me pretending to play music, with a small chair as an instrument, he bought me a little paper accordion."

Miha instantly began making music of his own—but with a twist. Not knowing better, he held the instrument backward, consequently learning to play the melody with his left hand instead of the right. A few years later, his would-be music teachers noticed this fact and understood that it gave him a head start in learning to play another instrument that would become his lifelong passion: the violin. That story would also instill in him a deep appreciation for the wisdom of trusting the often-unexpected magic in the twists and turns of life.

"Violin came to me by mistake, not by knowing violin or aspiring, but by the mystery of the *mistake* in life," Miha says.

His first teacher excelled at instilling enthusiasm, he says, but did a lousy job of conveying good technique. Even so, by the time he was six years old, Miha had already won regional violin competitions. At age eleven, he was sent to the big city of Maribor to compete—and heard a "real violinist" for the first time in his life, someone who truly understood the magic in the music and was passionate about getting it right.

"I was reduced to nothing," he recalls. "Nothing. That's when inspiration came that enabled me to not do what the other boys were doing around me. I determined to practice and practice and reach for the impossible."

It turned out that practice and mastery weren't the only "impossible" things Pogacnik would have to reach for. Quickly realizing he wanted more than his current teacher could deliver, he announced his intention to travel to the nearby city of Ljubljana to study with someone else.

It didn't matter that his teacher responded by throwing a music stand or that his otherwise supportive parents locked him in his room. He climbed out the window, made the trip, and was accepted into the school. For two years, he went twice a week by bus for the opportunity to learn. His first teacher there began the work of undoing all of his bad habits.

"He completely took me apart," Miha says. "I was below zero when I started over."

But start over he did. He pushed himself extremely hard, diving deep into the music. In the process, he laid the foundation for a philosophy that would guide him throughout his life: the ability to think like a "radical."

"Always I was radical. If you want to be a soloist, you have to be radical to yourself. You have to practice like mad. And of course, you have to learn how to practice. One can meditate and just repeat the word a billion times and nothing happens. In other words, one has to develop techniques and routines that will eventually bear fruit."

This radical path led him out of the East to Cologne, Germany, at age seventeen to study music on a prestigious scholarship for foreigners—then to the United States at twenty-four as a Fulbright Scholar.

A Hundred Years Behind

To become a soloist in the world of classical music is the dream of thousands of gifted performers and is the pinnacle of success. By his late twenties, Miha had captured the prize, well on his way to a long career among the elite musicians of the world. It was a stunning achievement for a boy from an isolated country who learned to play the wrong way on a paper accordion. It was also a source of deep internal crisis. It set the stage for a moment of decision that would cost him everything—and also, in magical fashion, deliver everything he has since come to value.

"As I started my career, I pretty soon noticed that the world in which you act as a violinist is about a hundred years behind the rest of the world," Miha says. "It's stuck in an organizational system in which you have to do certain things, you have to know certain people, and you have to win certain competitions. You play concerts and there are thousands who are waiting for you to be out of the system so they can come take your place."

What bothered him most was the self-serving nature of the entire structure. It offered no opportunity, he felt, to step outside the confines of the system "in order to become an element of social change, to really reach the situation into which the world has gotten itself." He knew that music had much more to offer than the status quo would allow—because he believed that it literally was much more than lifeless frequencies vibrating in the air. He knew it was *magic*.

"I have always been trying to unlock the mystery, why was music in the ancient cultures so powerful? Thousands of years ago, music was regarded as the most sacred and most power-ful element of society, and therefore you had to be bloody careful how you handled it. I wanted to know, what are the deeper secrets of musical magic that we have forgotten in the process of making it aesthetic and formal?"

So he turned his back on the life of comfort and prestige that all his hard work had earned him. He set out on a quest to be a musician of the highest quality he could possibly at-tain—and an agent of needed change in the world.

Go Against the Odds

The first leg of the journey took Miha in an unexpected direction—to a place that became for him a classroom of preparation for everything that would follow. He was invited to create a festival at the Camphill Village Residential Com-munity for adults with developmental disabilities.

Founded in 1961 on 615 acres in upstate New York, the organization was part of a growing American movement to challenge how society treats people with special needs. Though he didn't know it at the time, that mission fit per-fectly with his desire to create a model for music perfor-mance that invited audiences to do more than simply listen for intellectual stimulation. He wanted to make them deeply feel the music.

"Those people forced me to teach them how to listen, which to me seemed obvious," Miha recalls. "I said, 'What can you do? You just play and you listen.' They said, 'No, we don't understand.' The key question was how can I, as a per-former who goes full steam into a masterpiece, transfer that so that it goes beyond aesthetics, beyond beautiful music? How can I build a bridge? These people were my teachers."

To meet this challenge, Miha discovered anew how to be fully present when he played, to go beyond performance and become a "phenomenologist"—someone who studies the relationship between human consciousness and experience. The key idea in this philosophical discipline is that experience is intimately intertwined with intention and self-awareness. And it worked. A bond was created between him and his so-called "handicapped" audience that transcended anything he'd experienced before.

"That created an opportunity for people to start looking at the role of art in inner human development, spiritual development, which can be supported by immersing oneself deeply into the great arts," he says.

And it opened the door for what Miha calls his first "little festivals"—one-day events aimed at testing a bold idea: could he create a new kind of concert that involved his audiences as partners, not spectators, in crafting a musical experience?

It's a question that he has spent his life attempting to answer.

In April 1981, he held the first of many music festivals at the Chartres Cathedral in Chartres, France. In 1983, in the shadow of heightened Cold War tensions—when Europe was in turmoil over the deployment of U.S. Pershing missiles on German soil—Miha organized a festival in his home country of Slovenia. It was the first of its kind since the Iron Curtain had descended across the continent—and drew eight hundred people from Western Europe who travelled there to attend.

"It was the first time that the artists didn't just travel to give a concert—the audience traveled too, to be a part of social change," he says. "The idea was to go to places that are in distress and see what happens if you meet the locals in such a condition."

From there he organized weeklong festivals in Budapest, Prague, all over East Germany and the Soviet Union. Everywhere he went, concert halls were packed with locals and westerners alike, enabling a powerful grassroots cultural exchange. All of it involved hours and hours of work and expenses that seemed to only be met by magic.

But he never stopped thinking big. One trip involved renting seven ships and visiting towns all along the coast of the former Yugoslavia during the bloody war in the 1990s. Another trip filled a Trans-Siberian railway train with musicians and other cultural thinkers for a three-week long journey from Berlin to Ulan Bator, Mongolia.

"What I learned is that one should never give up," he says. "Go against all the odds. That has been confirmed over and over in my life. If you have a high inspiration, never mind that it doesn't show results immediately. Just keep going."

A Wall Comes Down

In 1989, the fall of the Berlin Wall changed everything— yet again—for Miha. Overnight, the ideals of freedom and

cultural cooperation that had fueled his festivals across Eastern Europe were replaced by a singular force: capitalism.

"In Eastern Europe, I saw people completely changing
their soul make-up of a Slavic kind of life in order to fit into
this globalized western kind of thinking," Miha remembers.
"Suddenly, there was not much meaning except surviving."

A stark example of this fundamental shift came in Dres-
den, East Germany. Before the wall fell, Miha gave a concert
there in a hall packed with people hungry to immerse in the
music. A year later, in the same place, only a handful showed
up. It was a wake-up call revealing a new reality and the challenge inherent in the composition of this new world: How
to form an economy that exists to serve the people, not the
other way around. Above all, Miha still believed the answer
lay in music and the other great arts.

65 —

"The arts represent the courtyard before you enter the
temple of transformation," he says. "They tune you up to that
frequency with which you can enter the temple of knowledge. I'm not just an activist to be active on the outside, but
I'm also working to create the inner capital, the spiritual capital that brings dynamic balance."

In perhaps the hardest life transition of all, Miha abandoned the festivals he had worked so hard to create over the
years—"threw them in the dust," as he likes to say. He started
over, not to oppose capitalism and its leaders, but to speak to
them through the medium of music, to inspire them to see
past the bottom line.

It's not easy work, nor is it easy for those who are touched by his message. At heart Miha has never stopped being a radical, and he pushes others to the radical life as well, come what may.

"When people ask me what is real inspiration, I say go to the mountain just after the lightning hits and have a look at what happens. You'll see all the smoldering trees and all the rest."

In other words, he says, don't be afraid of the kind of inspiration that burns down all that you think you know, so that something new can take its place. Don't be afraid to reinvent yourself as many times as it takes to follow your dream.

"We live in a very pragmatic time," he reflects. "We are not capable of grasping what idealism means, really. It's very rare to find people who have a blazing idealism. If you have very high ideals about what you'd like to achieve, then all of the setbacks don't kill them. Your ideals fuel resiliency and fire your passion, so you can start again."

CHAPTER 7

CLEAR THE DEBRIS FROM THE ROAD
For a Smoother Path Forward,
Get Rid of Obstacles and Obstructions

"A person often meets his destiny on the road he took to avoid it."
Jean de La Fontaine

In the ancient world, before a royal retinue set out on a journey, a contingent of servants would run ahead to clear the road of debris or obstructions, making the pathway safe for those who followed. That certainly made the trip smoother and also safer. A halted caravan was easy prey for bandits or enemies.

When you've set your sights on success, it is also wise to survey the landscape ahead and take stock of those things from your past or present life that might get in your way—by slowing you down, or worse, stopping you in your tracks.

In previous chapters, we've channeled our inertia, read the signs, acknowledged that resistance is futile, readied our vehicle, and charted a course. Now it's time to prepare the road ahead.

We want to see how we can best enjoy this exciting, scary and challenging journey on the road less traveled. How can we laugh at the situation, laugh at ourselves and smile over the insanity of the world we live in? How do we learn to laugh *with* others and not at them? How can we enjoy the serenity and peace of driving alone and appreciate our partner and like-minded friends who are along for the ride?

Let's explore proven strategies for how to do just that. These involve focusing on three elements as you look ahead: the Road, the Vehicle, and the Debris.

The Road

In the most literal sense, the road is "your chosen path toward your destination."

> Well the night's busting open
> These two lanes will take us anywhere
> We got one last chance to make it real
> To trade in these wings on some wheels
> Climb in back, heaven's waiting on down the tracks
> Oh-oh come take my hand, we're riding out tonight to case

the promised land
Oh-oh Thunder Road oh Thunder Road[1]

Bruce Springsteen, *Thunder Road*

Think about every road and path you've ever traveled. Often times, like life, they are filled with twists and turns and detours. You have red lights, green lights, turn signals, road construction signs, billboards, and untold other distractions. You pass familiar and unfamiliar places. Sometimes you encounter traffic or you're stuck behind a slow-moving truck.

Other times, you sail along at high speed. Often you travel alone with your own thoughts, sometimes in a van full of strangers. You watch for signs that you're going the right way or made a wrong turn. Some days the sun is shining, and other times it's cold, dark, and rainy.

In other words, no two journeys are precisely alike. Every path presents its own challenges and rewards. It is uniquely yours, and your job is to travel it courageously and decisively. The first step in doing that brings us to the second of our three elements.

The Vehicle

What is your car or rocket ship? Yourself, of course.

Let's face it, when it comes to our health, life happens. Issues arise. Problems come up. You would take your car in for a tune-up and oil change before setting out on a cross-country trip, right? In the same way, you should pay attention to the condition of your body—to protect it from breaking down and stranding you on the side of the road.

We only have one body, so we have to make the most of it. If you're not healthy before you begin, it's harder to get healthy along the way. You might already be facing health challenges today. Should you wait before you embark? Absolutely not! You'll have to continue your treatments and wellness regimen en route to your destination.

Maybe this is the time to go on the weight-loss program you've tried before, or get in better physical shape to help your mental state. Get that physical, blood-work, prostate test—and a complete check-up. It's also a fine time to lean on your spiritual background or religious beliefs to develop the clear, concentrated, present mind and spirit you'll need for the journey ahead.

The Debris

The obstacles in the road are both real and imagined. But you get to decide: clear the debris, drive around it, or ignore it and plow right through. In an actual journey, your intended path may be blocked by rocks, trees, branches, downed power lines, wild animals, road workers, ruts and landslides. These objects could represent guilt you have in your life for things said and done—or unsaid and undone. They are the anger, disappointment, heartache, resentment, inadequacies, jealousy and negative feelings you've felt and are still holding on to. You might hate the body you were given or have grown into. You might not like looking in the mirror at the person you've become.

The effort to clear debris from your road and press on toward your goal is worth all the pain, struggle and doubt. Why? Because the journey you're on right now—this expedition through life—is the only one you'll ever get. So go for it. Make the most of it!

> Against the grain should be a way of life
> What's worth the prize is always worth the fight
> Every second counts 'cause there's no second try
> So live like you'll never live it twice
> Don't take the free ride in your own life[2]
>
> Nickelback, *If Today Was Your Last Day*

All this sounds great, right? We all want to take the "free ride" in life, to clear the debris and allow nothing to stand in our way. But how do we do that? Here are three practical ways to get started:

1. Get your physical house in order—literally. Clean out your junk drawers. Simplify your life. Give stuff away. Ask yourself: Why am I keeping things that are just holding me down?

2. Get your financial house in order. Reduce or eliminate your debt. Cancel the subscriptions you're not really using. Meet with a financial planner and make sure your savings and investments are solid and secure.

3. Get your relationship house in order. Make sure you and your partner are stable and in sync. Confirm that he or she is up for the road trip ahead. If you have friends and family who you have not spoken to for years, call them up, make amends and move on.

71 —

Before I left for Everest, I did these very things. Of course, I'd had a physical and done all the training and preparation climbs I could do. I had my house cleaned, organized my finances, left an "in-case-of" envelope, and talked to my sons about what to do if I did not return. I got my divorce legally finalized. I talked to many of my friends and family before I left—and a few by satellite phone while I was there.

In hindsight, having seen the effects in a couple of climbers on mountains, I realize if I had not sorted relationship issues before I left, I would have been a mental mess much of the time while there. It would have weighed on me more than the pack I carried.

There is, however, no way to achieve perfection before embarking on our respective journeys. All we can do is clear more debris from the road by acknowledging our vulnerabilities and letting go of limiting beliefs so we can move forward. Though we hope to construct a life that will be perfect, it just is not possible. We end up trying to eliminate mistakes, but often we ignore our vulnerabilities and aim for perfection.

Curiously, however, the enemy of greatness is not failure but perfection. When we are open to the possibilities and recognize our strengths and weaknesses, we can then take appropriate risks to change our trajectory. If we stumble or hit a pile of debris in the road, we course correct. We keep moving forward.

A few years ago, Michelle and I were having dinner with a senior ex-colleague named Kim—Scottish, outspoken, direct and outrageously funny. As we discussed my career and what to do next, I told her all the reasons I could not do what I wanted to. In her Scottish brogue, she said, "Mitch, these are the stories you're telling yourself."

I looked at her, somewhat shocked, until what she said had sunk in. She was right! My excuses were just stories. After I cleared away that debris, I decided afterward to make a move in a different direction and have some scary and risky discussions with the management of my company. Six months later, we ended up moving to and working in Singapore in a position that I really wanted and was well suited for.

Keep It Simple

We often make the process of clearing debris from the road of our lives harder than it has to be—by struggling against what is. We say, "Why does this always happen to me?" Or, "I don't deserve this!" Instead, it is possible to simply acknowledge the obstacle, seek help in removing it and move on.

When debris that's out of your control blocks your journey toward your goal and dream, it is helpful not to overanalyze why it happened. I like to think of having a debris-removal crew standing by, ready for my emergency call to help get me out of this situation and on my way.

Sometimes this crew is busy helping others and does not come as fast as I wish they would, so I get frustrated. If it's a complex removal project, I try to break down the problem into smaller, bite-size pieces where the simplest answer is probably the right one. If it's truly chaotic, sometimes the best thing is just to get out of there, lick my wounds, not make the situation worse, and live to fight another day—after a good night's sleep. It's not always easy, but the simpler you make the solution, the easier it will be to clear the debris on your road.

Questions to Help You Climb Higher

1. What is the debris in your road right now? Is it physical, mental, or spiritual? Is it real or imagined?

2. How can you best remove it, and whom do you need to help you to do so? What beliefs, hard feelings and resentments are you harboring?

3. When can you start to clear things up and get your house in order? Where will you start?

Strategies for Success

Some tips on debris removal:

1. Recognize and document your debris. It is yours alone.

2. Make a list of those things in your physical, financial, and relationship house that need cleaning, sorting and resolving. Prioritize them and knock them off one at a time.

3. Prepare your personal road-clearing crew—and strategies for the inevitable rock falls and landslides. Remind yourself that this will be funny later—and if you can laugh in the moment, how great that would be.

Clearing the debris from the road is an integral part of any meaningful journey toward your dreams. The debris is there to test you along the way. If you can, call upon the "resistance is futile" mantra and know that the end result will make the challenges you have overcome that much sweeter. Remember that the best stories are always about the setbacks and obstacles we face, and how we overcame them through our will, resolve and goodness.

Finally, never forget that the debris you clear today makes the road smoother and safer for others as they embark on their own adventure.

CHAPTER 8

NO MISSED OPPORTUNITIES

When Her Dream Came Knocking,
Robin Hauser Reynolds Opened the Door

I n 2015, the prestigious Tribeca Film Festival premiered a documentary film called *CODE: Debugging the Gender Gap*, produced and directed by Robin Hauser Reynolds. By the time the screening ended and the lights came up, the audience had experienced a penetrating look at a social and economic issue of international importance: the dramatic lack of female programmers in the male-dominated technology industry.

Insightful writing, supported by beautiful imagery and music, made the film a shining example of cinematic excellence—a testament to Robin's professionalism and skill. By November 2016, *CODE* had screened in forty-two countries and won numerous awards.

Watching the film, it would be easy to imagine that Robin, fifty years old at the time of its release, had spent a lifetime working her way up in the filmmaking business, preparing for such an achievement. In reality, it might have come as a shock to moviegoers to learn that a mere six years earlier Robin was just about as far away from being a successful and celebrated filmmaker as possible.

Instead, she was stuck in what she considered to be a stifling marriage, convinced that her dreams all belonged in the realm of "missed opportunity." Though she'd begun her adult life armed with an MBA, and had embarked on a business career in Europe, full-time motherhood came along to displace all that.

"I was married to a man who wanted me at home, making sure there was dinner on the table and that I was waiting for him when he got off work or off the golf course," she recalls. "It was a very traditional marriage and I knew I wasn't happy with that, but I hung in there for the kids." Though she readily affirms that being a traditional mom is an honorable and valuable role, once her children were a bit older she was eager to explore the entrepreneurial gifts that lay dormant inside her.

Despite feeling trapped in a confining marriage, Robin admits that other facets of her life were far from "difficult."

She lived in a house on the water in one of the most prestigious zip codes in the country—Marin County, California, just north of San Francisco. She had ample time to devote to raising her two children and to numerous volunteer activities in the community. She travelled extensively on family vacations.

"I lived a beautiful life," she said. "I just wasn't fulfilled. I didn't feel like I was giving back enough. There were a lot of things I did in the community, but I didn't feel I was making a difference in the world."

That altruistic goal, to use her time and energy to make the world a better place, jostled in her mind with another latent desire that had slipped away over the years—to make a movie. The closest she had come was to become a still photographer, a hobby she pursued with passion. But her love of visual storytelling on film continued to smoulder beneath the surface.

Then something happened to fan the flames: She saw a documentary film called *Born into Brothels*, which told the story of children whose mothers were prostitutes in one of the toughest cities in India. Released in 2004, the film went on to win the Academy Award for Best Documentary Feature.

"I'd seen lots of documentary films, but there was something about this one that changed me," Robin recalls. "Sitting in the theater, I felt an intense longing to get involved in documentary filmmaking. But I sat there thinking, *I don't know how. I don't know if I can. Darn it, I've missed out on something I've always wanted to do.*"

That moment, seated in a darkened theater surrounded by strangers, became a turning point in Robin's life. Though she didn't know it at the time, the bittersweet longing she felt, the sense that her dream had slipped away, would become the fuel to help her break free of the bonds of previous limitations.

Step two would come many months later when another serendipitous event arose to test her misplaced belief that she'd missed the boat where her filmmaking dream was concerned. In 2010, a documentary crew literally arrived on the family's doorstep—but they hadn't come for Robin. They came to tell a story involving her daughter, Holland.

A Race to Remember

In 2010, sixteen-year-old Holland was a cross-country runner on the all-girls team at San Francisco University High School. That year, however, the team's coach, Jim Tracy, became the center of attention as the season progressed—for two reasons.

First, he was tied with a colleague as the "winningest" cross-country coach in California history, with eight state championship titles to his name.

Second, he'd just been diagnosed with ALS, also known as Lou Gehrig's disease, and the prognosis was grim. Now more than ever, the girls wanted to win. They wanted to give Tracy one more championship, the one that would put him in sole possession of the right to be called the best ever.

The state cross-country meet that year was held on an unseasonably cold and rainy morning in Fresno. Holland, the team's fastest runner, was within sight of turning the dream into reality with a win that would help deliver the championship—when she collapsed a few feet short of the finish line. A race official rushed to the side of the dehydrated and disoriented girl, but she refused to quit, crawling the remaining distance across the line on all fours.

The team would have narrowly won the title even if Holland had not finished the race, but the story of her gutsy effort—giving everything she had for her coach—became an international news sensation.

A short time later the film crew arrived in Marin County, asking the family's permission to tell the whole story in a feature-length documentary. Eager to become involved in the process, Robin took on the role of executive producer, raising money to fund the production. But as time went on, she became dissatisfied with the direction the project was taking and with what she considered to be the production's subpar quality.

"I had no interest in making the movie be about my daughter," she says. "But I wanted to have control over how she was personified. I also wanted to turn the story around and make sure the focus was on finding a cure for ALS."

In other words, her smouldering creative drive to make movies began to assert itself. In a matter of months, Robin had become the film's producer and director. *Running for Jim* went on to screen at twenty-two festivals worldwide and win fourteen awards.

81 —

Moment of Decision

The experience of making that film was both a dream come true for Robin and a nightmare of confronting the past choices that had kept her trapped for so long in an unfulfilling life. Fate had presented her with the opportunity she'd once believed would never come. But to claim it, she'd have to fight for what she believed—and live with the consequences.

The fiercest opposition she faced came from her now ex-husband, who claimed the film project was exploiting their daughter. That conflict forced Robin to make the decision she'd been avoiding for years between being true to herself and letting others chart the course of her life.

"I just had to know what I was doing and why, that my values and reasons for doing it were right, and to trust that when the film came out people would get that," she says. "I used that as fuel to become more determined to make the film and make it good."

Running for Jim also fueled her realization that, where she once had wanted simply "to make a film," now she was determined to be a "filmmaker" as a career and a way of life.

Robin recalls a pivotal moment sitting in the editing suite and watching a scene from Running for Jim come together. It was a dramatic re-enactment of a key moment in Jim Tracy's childhood—running with his siblings on the track between horse races at various California venues. It was the first such scene she'd designed and directed by herself.

"The scene in the film produced the same feeling I had when watching Born into Brothels," she says. "The convergence of the visuals and the music built up a swell of emotion, and it sank in on me that I was actually doing what not that long ago I had thought was out of reach. It was an incredible moment."

Suddenly, the doubts that had plagued her a few years earlier—*I don't know how! I don't know if I can!*— disappeared. From there she produced and directed *CODE*, which found its success at Tribeca Film Festival just four years later, the same year she separated from her husband.

"I named my production company Unleashed Productions for a reason," she says. "I feel that I have unleashed passion now for making cause-based films that make a difference, influence people and try to promote change for the better."

83 —

No Stopping Now

Along the way, Robin has had ample opportunity to share what she's learned with other people struggling to overcome opposition—no matter the source—and follow their dream.

"I tell them to commit, believe, and push forward. It's important to really believe you belong in the room pursuing your dreams," she explains. "Say it out loud: 'I'm going to run the San Francisco Marathon.' Now I'm committed to it. It's scary, but it also validates your intention, and then you can move forward."

It's no accident that the cause-based stories Robin is most drawn to tell involve freeing people—women in particular—

from social and economic barriers to equal treatment. She believes that change begins when people collectively "push back" against all kinds of mistreatment, whether blatant or nuanced. These days she spends her time producing and directing a film called *Bias*—an examination of unconscious prejudice and how it affects our behavior socially and in the workplace. Mention future films on her horizon, and she bubbles with possible subjects.

"I would never have ended my marriage to pursue my dream of becoming a full-time filmmaker had I not had the voice in my head and the feeling in my gut that kept telling me, *It's now or never.*"

CHAPTER 9

FIND YOUR SPIRITUAL CENTER

Honor Your Beliefs and You'll Gain Inspiration
for the Journey

"You have to grow from the inside out. None can teach you, none can make you spiritual. There is no other teacher but your own soul."
Swami Vivekananda

O ver the years I've often heard people say, "I'm not religious, but I am spiritual." Or, "I don't participate in organized religion, but I do have a rich spiritual life."

Personally, I was fuzzy on the distinction between these two concepts—until I found a helpful definition on biographyonline.net: "*Religion* usually entails adhering to a certain dogma or belief system. *Spirituality* places little importance on intellectual beliefs, but is concerned with growing into and experiencing the divine consciousness." I'd add that *spirituality* is something or someone you believe in while religion is something that you belong to.

Ultimately, it doesn't matter what words you choose to describe this ineffable part of the human experience. What's important is to understand that finding your spiritual center—regardless of the path you take to get there—is an *essential* step toward reaching your goals, fueling your passions and enjoying the journey to the fullest.

Why? First, it gives you hope and inspires you to keep going against all odds. The rational, scientific person looks only at facts and figures. Athletes help win big games through sheer willpower (combined with their skills and experience). There will be days in your journey when you wonder why you're fighting so hard. Faith is what will see you through. Sometimes you will have to take a leap of faith and trust in your higher power.

And we all need something or someone to believe in. George Carlin once said, "You know who I pray to? Joe Pesci. Two reasons: First of all, I think he's a good actor, okay? To me, that counts. Second, he looks like a guy who can get things done. Joe Pesci doesn't [fool] around. In fact, Joe Pesci came through on a couple of things that God was having trouble with."

The second reason spirituality is your ally on the journey to achieve your dreams can be summed up in a single word: Purpose. We are all here for a reason. We were not put on the earth just to procreate, pay bills and die. Mother Teresa (now Saint Teresa of Calcutta) famously said, "We ourselves feel that what we are doing is just a drop in the ocean. But the ocean would be less because of that missing drop."

To realize your higher purpose—your unique contribution to the ocean of life—you must allow a higher power to guide your quest and help you along the way. This power can be anything or anyone you believe in—your God or gods, or the belief that God resides in all of us, and we are all connected to each other and to the energy of the universe. There are many ways to express these beliefs—in silent meditation or prayer or in a mosque, temple, or church.

Almost 99 percent of the human body is made up of six elements: oxygen, carbon, hydrogen, nitrogen, calcium, and phosphorus. Only about 0.85 percent is composed of another five elements: potassium, sulfur, sodium, chlorine, and magnesium. All are necessary for life. All come from our planet, the solar system and the universe. We understand that we're made of elements, how cell-splitting works, and the science and mechanics of making a human being.

Some have suggested that all of this functions with no more magic or mystery than a cosmic clock—gears and wheels spinning according to cold rules of physics and chemistry. Any father or mother will tell you, however, that holding your child for the first time is a *spiritual* experience. The hopes and dreams we feel in that moment for this new life transcend mere biology, because birth is a miracle and life is a miracle.

Spirituality and religion can help bring us comfort, peace, hope, goodness, tolerance, acceptance . . . all toward becoming a better person along the way. Some people say that religion is the path to God; spirituality is also a path to God. They differ only in approach.

As Indian spiritual teacher Sri Chinmoy said, "The essence of religion: Fear God and obey God. The quintessence of spirituality: Love God and become another god."

Many Paths

Alcoholics Anonymous (AA) is an international mutual-support fellowship founded in 1935 by Bill Wilson and Dr. Bob Smith in Akron, Ohio. The group's primary purpose is to help alcoholics "stay sober and help other alcoholics achieve sobriety." AA was originally based on the Christian faith, and members were required to share its beliefs to achieve sobriety. Over time, however, AA and the twelve-step program it uses evolved to include the idea that any "higher power" could be a source of strength to an individual suffering from addiction.

One study found an association between regular participation in AA meetings and increased spirituality—and a decrease in the frequency and intensity of alcohol use. The authors concluded, however, that though spirituality was an important mechanism of behavioral change for some alcoholics, it was not the only effective one.

That's because the study also revealed AA to be effective at helping agnostics and atheists. Since the mid-1970s, a number of "agnostic" or "no-prayer" AA groups sprung up across the U.S., Canada and other parts of the world. These groups hold meetings that allow alcoholics to freely express their doubts or disbelief that spirituality will help their recovery, and forgo opening or closing prayers.

My parents were Jewish of the Conservative branch, closer to the Reform end of the spectrum than Orthodox believers. Our family believed in God, but we were not particularly religious. We went to the synagogue for all the major holidays, and my mom loved to cook for the big ones: Passover, Rosh Hashanah, Yom Kippur and Hanukkah. Neither of my parents could speak Hebrew, but my dad liked to read the transliterations in the book of Seder.

89 —

They sent me to Hebrew school when I was young, and I was proud on the day of my Bar Mitzvah—standing in front of my family and friends at age thirteen, reading the old Hebrew from the Torah. I remember the tribal atmosphere I felt in the synagogue, and the sense of belonging. I understood that Jewish people had been persecuted for centuries, the target of prejudice through time for being "cheap" or bankers or lawyers. Most of all, I knew that millions of us were killed during the Holocaust. We *were* members of a tribe.

My Jewish education never included criticism of Christianity, Islam or any other religion. The synagogue was a gathering place, a community honoring a common belief. We were taught to follow certain practical rules, such as: Don't eat meat with milk and don't eat pork. But mostly we studied deeper concepts and commandments: Do unto others what you would have them do to you; honor your father and your mother; don't lie, cheat, steal, or murder.

Looking for More

I couldn't have described it then, but I've come to realize something was missing for me in that religious approach to spirituality—an answer to the perplexing question of purpose. Why do we exist? What were we put on earth for? What is the way to live a better life and make life better for others?

For the next twenty-five years, I neither practiced the faith, nor for the most part even acknowledged that I was Jewish. I can't say that religion or spirituality were even in my mindset. I focused instead on raising a family, advancing in my career and improving my golf game.

That changed the day my oldest son, Jeremy, came home one afternoon during his senior year in high school and announced that he did not believe in God. The comment came innocuously, in the middle of a conversation, not as a heartfelt protest or rebellion—just as a statement of fact. My first thoughts were of anger, disappointment and bargaining.

"What?" I responded. "How can you not believe in God?"

I tried to argue with him, which seemed only to strengthen his resolve. I wondered if I had done wrong in raising him without religion and not having him enjoy a Bar Mitzvah of his own. It soon emerged that he had been reading Ayn Rand, and her ideas in books like *The Fountainhead* and *Atlas Shrugged* had shaped his views.

In an effort to understand, I read the books, which I also found instructive in some ways. I did not agree with all of the concepts, but they helped me see where Jeremy was coming from, where I had been and how to put all of this in context. Still being somewhat ignorant, I started to label myself as an atheist at worst or an agnostic at best. To be truthful, I was afraid of alienating God, worried that he would take vengeance on me in some way. So I wanted to hedge my bets.

During this time, I read Carl Sagan's *The Demon-Haunted World: Science as a Candle in the Dark*. In this book, he tried to explain this seeming conflict between our rational brains and religious beliefs. He wrote:

> Science is not only compatible with spirituality; it is a profound source of spirituality. When we recognize our place in an immensity of light-years and in the passage of ages, when we grasp the intricacy, beauty, and subtlety of life, then that soaring feeling, that sense of elation and humility combined, is surely spiritual. So are our emotions in the presence of great art or music or literature, or acts of exemplary selfless courage such as those of Mohandas Gandhi or Martin Luther King, Jr. The notion that science and spirituality are somehow mutually exclusive does a disservice to both.[1]

91 —

I have lived with Baptists in the Bible Belt in Texas, with Lutherans in Sweden, and with Muslims, Hindus, Buddhists, and Christians in Malaysia, Indonesia and Singapore. Three decades after that conversation with my son, I woke up to the possibility of what spirituality could bring to our lives and that we're all on a grand journey of discovery—individually and together. There are many ways to conceive of the higher power that accompanies us, whether we acknowledge it or not.

John Lennon once said, "I believe in God, but not as one thing, not as an old man in the sky. I believe that what people call God is something in all of us. I believe that what Jesus and Mohammed and Buddha and all the rest said was right. It's just that the translations have gone wrong."

The Power of Practice

How do we reconcile our scientific, fact-based thinking with our spiritual beliefs? The answer lies in what we choose to believe and how we set about reinforcing those beliefs in our daily lives.

When we see a beautiful sunset, flowers in bloom, or snow on a distant mountain, we understand that these are mere photons of light captured by our eyes and translated by our brains into an image. Science has taught us it is a purely physical process. We have to appreciate, though, that there is symmetry in the world, natural order, precision and balance that goes beyond atomic building blocks to something more meaningful. That something is created and cared for by a higher power—the same power that is there for you during your life quest and the constant changes you have to navigate.

This spirit, energy and life force will indeed propel you through the best and worst days of your journey toward your passions. Keeping your everyday thoughts in line with your purest intentions will help make it possible. The imaginative power of the mind allows us to visualize both the perfect golf shot and standing on top of a mountain. We gain expertise and skills through training; we achieve greatness through visualization.

You are not a computer or a robot. You are the captain of your ship, letting data *plus* mindfulness guide your decisions. A computer thinks in binary terms (zeros and ones), but it has no dreams and no hopes. It does not feel passion, love or intimacy; it believes in nothing except for data. A computer follows no one. Humans, with all of our faults and "software" bugs, get to experience and feel what it is like to fall deeply in love, cross a finish line, paint a masterpiece and see our child graduate.

Of course, we also must experience the darkest emotions of loss, death, illness and injustice. Even in these things, though, there is growth and the wisdom necessary for following your dreams. As the Quran says, "So verily with the hardship there is relief."

93 —

Many times in my life I have prayed for my children, for colleagues or friends, or just to stay alive (though I'm happy to say I've never prayed to Joe Pesci). Affirmations and meditation are not just for Buddhists or New Agers; they're time-proven techniques to help us achieve peace, tranquility and greatness. On your journey, there are many tools available to help you.

I once worked for a man named Darren, who is one of the most technically brilliant people I know. He designed and built some of the most extreme networking boxes in the world, to enable data transfer between machines over a terabit (trillion bit) connection. Once, in a senior-level customer meeting, he told Ron, a senior member of our management team, that he could "make his blood go backward."

Puzzled, Ron said, "What do you mean? That's impossible!"

Darren explained that he practices the ancient Chinese art of Qigong and that his claim was indeed possible. The conversation then moved on to more mundane topics such as revenue growth—but that day I became fascinated with the concept of Qigong.

The name of the practice is derived from two Chinese words. Qi (pronounced "chee") is usually translated to mean *the life force or vital energy that flows through all things in the universe.* Gong (pronounced "gung") means *accomplishment or skill that is cultivated through steady practice.* Together, Qigong means cultivating energy, and it is a system practiced for health maintenance, healing and increasing vitality.

I continue to be fascinated by the realms of science and spirituality and what our bodies and minds can do on a daily basis with our wills. We can learn from within or from others such as the Center for Spiritual Living in San Jose, California.

Let me leave you with the mission statement of CSL San Jose, where my friend Susan Overland serves (she was featured earlier in this book). Let these words inspire you to find your own spiritual center as you embark on your journey.

> We believe that the Universe is fundamentally spiritual, and that it has intelligence, purpose, beau-

ty and order. Our beliefs are in harmony with the basic tenets of all the world's great religions and for that reason we honor all paths to God. Whether we call it God, spirit, energy, or Universal Intelligence, every person, place and thing emanates from this spiritual universe. We believe this Universal Intelligence is within us, as well as around us, and that we are conscious of it. We believe that God is a loving intelligence, operating in and through all life, never separate from anyone or anything.

When you open your heart and mind to the wonder of the universe and God—however you define them—you energize your potential for achieving greatness for yourself and for others.

Questions to Help You Climb Higher

1. Are you living a good, honest, truthful, regret-free life—while trying to help others?

2. Are you open to the possibilities of science and the universe coexisting on your behalf?

3. Are you willing to set aside your own preconceived notions of unnatural forces and energy and faith to enable your personal growth goals?

Strategies for Success

How do you find and harness your spiritual center? Consider these ideas:

1. Realize your thoughts have energy. Make a practice of keeping your thoughts positive. Don't let them sabotage your mission when they tend toward the negative. There are scientific studies that prove the beneficial health effects of positive thinking and laughter.

2. Remember this is not all about you. A side effect of changing your life to meet your goals and aspirations can and should positively impact others along the way. Stay focused on your higher purpose with your higher power.

3. Recite the Serenity Prayer often. This prayer has a place in AA and in our pursuit of passionate purpose in life: "God grant me the serenity to accept the things I cannot change; courage to change the things I can; and wisdom to know the difference" (crafted by the brilliant Reinhold Niebuhr).

CHAPTER 10

SEEING THE BIG PICTURE
IN SMALL PLACES

Molecular Biologist Richard Ebstein Turned "Game
Over" into "Game On"

Only a handful of scientists can say their research has made the front page of the *New York Times*—and Dr. Richard Ebstein is among them. That puts him in elite company normally reserved for Nobel Prize winners or medical miracle workers.

Richard is neither, but in the mid-1990s he led a team of researchers that captured the world's attention by providing evidence of a novel idea: that an individual's personality is determined, at least in part, by his or her genetic makeup. It was the first time anyone had presented empirical evidence that DNA—the complex and unique genetic code contained in every cell in our bodies—could determine psychological traits as well as physical ones. Genetic blueprints, Richard and his team hypothesized, go beyond eye color and body type to influence whether a person is introverted or extroverted, adventurous or risk-averse, impulsive or overly cautious.

In particular, Richard demonstrated a link between certain variants in a "dopamine receptor gene" and what psychologists call "novelty-seeking" behavior. The popular press got wind of the research after a paper describing the finding was published in the prestigious scientific journal *Nature Genetics*.

"My brother-in-law, who was living in New Jersey at the time, called me and said, 'Dick, you won't believe this, but your name is in an article in the *New York Times*!'" Richard recalls. "That was the first I'd heard of it, and for about three weeks I was on a high. It was the most exciting period of my life, scientifically, at least for my ego. But after a month, the newspapers moved on to something else, and I went back to work in the laboratory."

Even so, Richard describes the discovery as a turning point in the modern study of human behavioral genetics. It opened the door on a whole new way of understanding why people behave as they do, what drives their decision-making and what that knowledge may contribute to our pursuit of a better society. It eventually led him to a post at the National University of Singapore, where he joined a team of behavioral economists and game theorists on the cutting edge of a brand-new field of study called "genoeconomics."

Richard's breakthrough was also the direct result of a colossal *failure*.

Game Over

More than three decades earlier, in the mid-1980s, Richard was at Yale University working toward a Ph.D. in molecular biology. The idea of deciphering human DNA in any detail—much less matching specific genes to particular traits—was met with skepticism by most scientists.

"It was kind of the *zeitgeist* of the time," he says. "One of our professors—and these were really smart guys—said to us, 'We'll never be able to understand how DNA codes for everything, because it's a complicated structure and we have no way of breaking it down into its component parts. It looks like an impossible task.'"

101 —

It took about ten years for that prediction to be proved false. A fast-moving revolution in technology and theoretical understanding made it possible to begin "mapping" the genome with a high degree of accuracy.

Of course, the structure of the human genome is complicated—containing about three billion DNA "base pairs"—combinations made up of just four basic "letters" in the genetic alphabet. Nearly all of that code is identical from one person to another, differing by only about 0.1 percent. By comparison, human beings differ genetically from our closest cousins—chimpanzees and bonobos—by about 4 percent.

That rate of variation between individual people may seem small, but to scientists like Richard, it's enough to prompt the question: Might it be possible to link specific gene "variants" to identifiable traits in individual people?

Once technology and technique caught up, Richard recalls, researchers were almost uniformly concerned with how this knowledge might shed light on the causes of disease and pathology—including mental illness. He was among them.

"I was interested in psychiatry and in looking for biological markers and explanations for major mental illnesses that would help doctors better diagnose people who were ill," Richard says. He spent months in Germany learning the necessary techniques from researchers there, then returned to his lab in Jerusalem with a lofty goal: To establish a link between schizophrenia and a specific gene variant related to a dopamine receptor in the brain.

Up until then, the most effective drugs for treating schizophrenia were all associated with dopamine and with that particular receptor, making it a natural choice. He and his psychiatrist colleague painstakingly designed his study. He and his team carefully collected and analyzed data over the next year. The project attracted considerable attention by others in the field who were eager to see the results.

"In those days, it was all kind of new, and everybody was following it," Richard recalls. "And in the end, I got nothing. It was very frustrating. It seemed like a great idea, but at the end of the year, we analyzed the data and found no relationship between this gene I'd been working on and schizophrenia. It was a game-over situation."

Richard admits that one possible response when we encounter a moment like that is to "move on" and find something else to do. In the world of research, that's particularly tempting, since a scientist's reputation can be severely damaged by refusing to accept apparently conclusive results.

"But I have a kind of creative way of thinking," Richard says. "It bothered me that, here I've got all these instruments and tools for solving a problem, but the problem I picked didn't work."

Perhaps he'd heard the old adage that failure is nothing more than a right answer looking for a different question. Maybe he was just plain stubborn. In any case, he kept mulling over his results until a pivotal insight struck him.

"I wondered, from an evolutionary standpoint, why do we have these variants at all? It's not related to mental illness, but there must be some explanation as to why we bother keeping it in our population."

That's when Richard had a "very good thought," he says with a mischievous chuckle. "It occurred to me that maybe the gene is not related to mental illness, but it is related to human personality, normal personality," he explains. "There were these basic personality traits that psychologists had been studying for donkey's years, but nobody had tried to link them to a specific gene. Nobody is looking at normal traits because everybody is interested in mental illness, myself included. It was a real 'Aha' moment."

Richard went back to the lab and in collaboration with Robert Belmaker, a psychiatrist at Ben Gurion University in Be'er Sheva, Israel, designed a different kind of experiment using the same tools as before—and this time found a significant link between the dopamine gene and "adventuresome" behavior, as measured by standard "pencil and paper" psychological questionnaires.

In a lucky turn of events, a group of researchers in America happened to have a pool of unanalyzed data that could provide the essential ingredient prestigious publications are looking for before printing new research: replication. The lab at the National Institutes of Health in Maryland found the same significant link—and Richard was on his way to the front page of the *New York Times* as one of the discoverers of the "adventure gene."

A Question of Altruism

Having opened the door to the study of genetic influence on normal human psychology, Richard kept going and shifted his attention to a personality trait that had bugged him for a while: altruism.

To explain the problem, he tells a hypothetical story.

"A guy is drowning in a river and you hear this cry for help. You say, 'I feel the need to help,' so you jump in the river and pull him out. You're a hero and you'll be on CNN the next day. But over the course of eons of time, a certain number of times, the guy who has this gene, who jumps in the water, he's going to drown."

The significance of that, to a biologist, is that drowning reduces the chances of that gene surviving in the population over huge stretches of time. It's the whole "survival of the fittest" thing.

"The genes ought to spread for the guy who stands by and says, 'Oh, the poor bastard is drowning.' And the genes should disappear for the guy who jumps in to be brave. And yet, both Darwin and Adam Smith realized that despite this genetic push toward survival, humans *are* generous and altruistic. The question is, why?"

That became the foundation for Richard's next set of experiments—and the source of profound conclusions about what our genetics can teach us about ourselves and how to live well with each other in society.

To begin, he designed another research protocol using standard pencil-and-paper questionnaires to rate a person's general altruism and then compare those findings with the presence or absence of a particular gene. The survey was the standard approach among psychologists at the time. The first identifiable trend to arise was a link between religion and altruism.

"The participants were mostly Israeli students, and it became clear that those who reported active religious affiliation also tended to display more altruistic behavior," Richard recalls.

However, it didn't take long for someone to point out the flaw in the process.

"This was a period in world history when the Soviet Union had just collapsed. A lot of Soviet Jews had emigrated and some had come to Israel. These were very smart people, but they also tended to be cynical, because of all they'd been through."

One such emigre was working in Richard's lab. She made a passing comment one day that changed the course of his research—and eventually led him to Singapore.

"These religious people are not more altruistic than the typical person," she told Richard. "They just make believe, so if you ask them, they know how to answer the question. But basically they're not any better than anybody else."

In other words, people could—and would—cheat.

That stopped Richard in his tracks and sent him in search of better way to measure altruism than simply asking people to describe themselves. It didn't take long to find the solution in a whole different field of study—using behavioral economic paradigms.

The Dictator Game

Across the campus at Ben Gurion University, some psychologists and economists trying to understand why and how people make decisions had already cracked the problem of accurately measuring altruism. The answer? *Incentivized* choice using behavioral economics "games."

"Instead of asking people what they're like, because they may lie or may not even know, economists say we have to incentivize the choices people make," Richard says. "If there's money involved, people will put their mouth where their pocket is."

In particular, researchers were using something called the Dictator Game developed by psychologist Daniel Kahneman, winner of a Nobel Prize in Economics. The game's premise is remarkably simple. One player, the "dictator," gets to decide how to divide a small pot of money between himself or herself and the only other player, an entirely passive "recipient." The money is real, and they both get to keep their share. There are no other incentives or penalties to influence the decision. The dictator's only reason for not keeping the cash for himself is to benefit the other person—and the percentage he chooses to give away is a reliable measure of relative altruism.

"It's a very clean laboratory-based approach," Richard says. "If you make them play an incentivized game, you get a better insight into what their prejudices are and what they really think."

With that data in hand, Richard was ready to start matching the findings to the presence or absence of certain gene variants. Once again, the results showed a significant link between the two—though Richard is quick to point out the limitations of the conclusion. In particular, he evokes the debate over whether people are most influenced by "nature" (genetics) or "nurture" (environment).

"Most people today in my profession would say it's half and half. We're 50 percent hardwired and 50 percent affected by environment. Everybody should be happy, because the people who think genetics play a large role are right, but the people who think it's about the environment are also right. It's very rabbinical," he adds with a chuckle.

In other words, an individual's genetic makeup may shape their choices, but they in no way "control" them.

A Biological Basis for Tolerance

That conclusion begs the question: What does Richard feel he has learned from his years of research into the genetic basis for human behavior? Again, a story is handy to help explain.

"I had grown up in a bubble, in a lower middle-class Brooklyn Jewish neighborhood. We were all academically oriented. I went to good schools and hung out most of my life with smart achievers. I got a little prejudiced thinking that we were the elite. I thought, *we're the people running the world, and that's what we need—more people like me.*"

This academic stratification only increased as he progressed through college. But in 1968, Richard made a fateful decision to leave the U.S. for Israel. The Vietnam War was at its height, and the Israelis had just won the Six-Day War a year earlier. He felt drawn to emigrate—perhaps demonstrating the presence in himself of a strong "novelty-seeking" gene. A couple of years after his arrival, he was drafted into the Israeli army and put to work in the engineering corps. He readily admits that put an end to feeling he lived in an elite "bubble."

"The big shock about that attitude came when I went into the Israeli army, and I discovered that my intellectual talents weren't always so helpful. When I learned to take apart an M-16 rifle blindfolded, or to clean a heavy machine gun, it turned out I wasn't that good at it," he says with a laugh.

He learned to appreciate the value of diversity then and the necessity of relying on all kinds of people with all kinds of talents and skills.

"Sure, I'm good at some things, but so are other people. And you wouldn't want a world with just me in it, because the machine gun would jam. We wouldn't make it. You can be smart, but if the machine gun doesn't work when you need it, you're finished."

Drawing on his years of scientific research, Richard sums up his advice to others in two words: Know yourself.

Understanding that our personality is in some measure "hardwired" into our genetics, he believes, helps clarify the task of self-improvement.

"If you realize that a personality trait, say risk aversion and anxiety, is at least partially hardwired, that means it's probably going to be hard to change. And therefore maybe you have to work a little harder at it. It's not written in stone but may take more effort to overcome."

That awareness also leads to his final conclusion—that we need to lighten up and let diversity be what it is.

"People are different. One shoe won't fit everybody. And that's good."

CHAPTER 11

FAILURE IS A FANTASTIC TEACHER …
AND SO IS SUCCESS

Learn Life Lessons Whenever and However They Show Up

"Only those who dare to fail greatly can ever achieve greatly."
Robert F. Kennedy

Psychologists tell us we learn the most from our failures—and that's true. It is also possible to learn from our successes, but the wisdom we garner from falling short is often the most meaningful and memorable.

Here's a good definition of failure: "When you attempt something and the desired result is less than what you expected." But just because an outcome does not live up to your expectations does not mean it had nothing to offer you. Quite the contrary.

Failure is just a word, a label we put on ourselves that carries all sorts of negative connotations. Our sports-obsessed culture has trained us to think that success and failure are like a light switch that's either on or off. A team either wins or loses, with nothing in between and no satisfying way to see the benefit of losing.

Together, let's explore some vital questions:

- What if the truth is not so clear-cut?

- What if failure is just a myth that has more to do with our personal and cultural preconceptions than it does with reality?

- What if the value of failure lies in our willingness to change how we look at it?

For example, when my friend Paula "failed" to reach the summit of Mt. Everest, she climbed to an altitude of more than twenty-eight thousand feet. At the moment she was forced to turn back, she had climbed higher than 99.9999 percent of the people on this planet ever have or will. Seen this way, it's hard to view that as a "failure" in the negative way we normally use the word.

On my first attempt to climb a mountain—Mt. Baker in Washington State—our rope team had ascended to over ten thousand feet when the guide stopped and said she was turning us around. We were not going to reach the summit that time. Knowing we were headed home, one member of our team, Jerry, got angry and threw rocks at the mountain.

Paula was sad and cried. And I felt determination building in myself to be better next time, though I was also angry at myself and sad for our "failure." Yes, I knew the weather had gone bad and parts of our intended path were not accessible. But being honest with myself, I also knew that I was not in the best physical shape and lacked the right equipment, skills and experience to be successful.

We lived to climb another day, and "failure" allowed me to be better prepared the next time out. If we had made a successful summit on my first attempt, I might have thought it was easy and not taken the necessary steps for improvement. When we don't initially get to where we want to be, we're often even more empowered and equipped to succeed in the next phase, *if* we can absorb and process the lessons from our past experiences.

113 —

A real danger arises when you experience an outcome that is "less than expected" and conclude that you yourself are a "failure." You might take it personally and see it as evidence of a character defect or that you simply aren't good enough. You reinforce that fallacy with your language when you say that failure is your "fault." This is especially true the more time, energy and money you have invested in the endeavor.

Misinterpreting failure in this way can lead to any number of excuses that might stop you in your tracks on your journey toward your dreams.

Failure Can Be an Excuse to Quit

Writing in *Forbes* magazine, Ektarina Walter says,

> It seems that failure tends to be more public than success. Or at least that's what we perceive it to be. We fret it, we try to avoid it, and we question ourselves every time we have unconventional ideas. But the simple truth is, no great success was ever achieved without failure. It may be one epic failure. Or a series of failures—such as Edison's 10,000 attempts to create a light bulb or Dyson's 5,126 attempts to invent a bag-less vacuum cleaner. But, whether we like it or not, failure is a necessary stepping stone to achieving our dreams.[1]

In other words: Don't quit now! You could be almost there! Think about the following scenarios:

- A scientist performs hundreds of "failed" experiments . . . until she finds the right combination of chemical ingredients and other conditions and discovers the disease-fighting compound.

- A salesperson experiences dozens of cold-calling hang-ups, door-slams in his face, offers not accepted . . . until he finally gets the big order.

- A woman keeps dating for years, "kissing many frogs" . . . and then finds the loving, intimate, trusted relationship she has been longing for, her "prince."

- A job seeker sends out countless résumés, receives numerous rejections or no-replies, and goes on dozens of interviews . . . and at last lands the job at the company meant for her.

In these scenarios, do you think that if any one of these people had gotten a "yes" or "success" on the first try that they would have appreciated the victory as much as if they had not "failed" at first? I doubt it.

The very best hitters in baseball have a batting average of around .300. That means they are called out 70 percent of the time—seven out of every ten times at bat! Yet that's good enough to earn them millions of dollars every year. Barry Bonds holds the lifetime homerun record in Major League Baseball with 762 hit over 22 years. But he also struck out 1,539 times.

115 —

Most of the MLB leaders in homeruns are also the leaders in strikeouts. We could deduce that "if you don't swing for the fences, you're not swinging hard enough, and you're bound to strike out more often than you hit one out." But you then have to keep swinging and make adjustments to your batting style, stride and tempo to decrease the ratio.

Failure Can Be an Excuse to Blame Others

When something goes "wrong," we are tempted to blame somebody or something—other people, our parents, the government, the weather, the market, or our teammates—rather than be introspective and take a clinical view of the failure. We also love to play the "what-if" game: *If only I'd been stronger. . . . If only he was a better husband. . . . If only I had been born into a wealthy family.*

These are not helpful thoughts, unless they reveal how you can do better next time.

The Dalai Lama says, "To be aware of a single shortcoming within oneself is more useful than to be aware of a thousand in somebody else. Rather than speaking badly about people and in ways that will produce friction and unrest in their lives, we should practice a purer perception of them, and when we speak of others, speak of their good qualities."[2]

I'm drawn to the story of Elon Musk and SpaceX. Musk was severely bullied throughout his childhood. He was once hospitalized when a group of boys threw him down a flight of stairs and then beat him until he blacked out. In 1999, Musk cofounded X.com, an online financial services and email payment company, with $10 million from the sale of a previous company. One year later, the company merged with Confinity, which had a money transfer service called Pay-Pal. Musk was ousted in 2000 from his role as CEO due to disagreements with company leadership—but in 2002, Pay-Pal was acquired by eBay for $1.5 billion in stock, of which Musk received $165 million.

That year, he founded SpaceX. It took almost seven years, but in September 2008, SpaceX's Falcon 1 rocket became the first privately funded liquid-fuelled vehicle to put a satellite into earth's orbit. On May 25, 2012, the SpaceX Dragon vehicle docked with the International Space Station, making history as the first commercial company to launch and berth a vehicle to the ISS.

But by July 2015, Musk and SpaceX had experienced disaster when their ISS resupply rocket failed and exploded during take-off—not once but three times in a few short months. This happened after the company had achieved a flawless safety record over the previous seven years. A sense of complacency had settled over SpaceX after its many years of success, Musk said.

But rather than lash out at others, he has turned the failures into an opportunity to improve company accountability and communication. Before every launch, he sends a company-wide email asking whether anyone can think of any possible reason to hold off, and if so, to call him on his cell phone or send an email.

"By the twentieth time I sent that email, it just seemed like, 'There's Elon being paranoid again.' Maybe it didn't resonate with the same force," he said. "But I think now everyone at the company appreciates how difficult it is to get rockets to orbit successfully, and I think we'll be stronger for it."

In April 2016—after five attempts in fifteen months to land one of its rocket boosters on a drone ship—SpaceX successfully landed the first stage of its Falcon rocket. This was the first time in history such a feat had been achieved by an orbital rocket.[3]

Failure Can Be an Excuse to Give in to Denial and Anger

In her groundbreaking book *On Death and Dying*, Elizabeth Kübler-Ross postulated that people who suffer a loss experience five stages of grief. The stages are denial, anger, bargaining, depression and acceptance. I believe we all go through these steps when we "fail" at a relationship, job or important goal.

Suppose you take a role in a company where deep down you know you're not a good fit. Or perhaps it's the wrong industry for you or the culture does not suit you. Maybe you can't get along with your boss or you have no support network. All of this can be compounded by personal missteps and lost opportunities to achieve what you were tasked to do.

This can happen whether you're the CEO of the company or working at an entry-level position. You can hope things will get better, but you also know that "hope is not a strategy." You know that despite whatever you try, you're just delaying the inevitable. I should know—it happened in my first job at age sixteen and again decades later.

When the time comes and you are given notice by your company, at first you'll be in denial. "This can't be happening to me!" You will then get angry, very angry, at the injustice of the situation, your horrible teammates, or bad luck. You then might try to bargain with the Human Resources department or your boss for a different position or more time to prove yourself. You'll then move into the depression phase, where you might have some hard drinking days, lethargy, and hiding away from the rest of the world after your "failure."

In time—and the length here is important—you will move into acceptance, which I also call the *determination* phase. You decide that no matter what happened, you had some personal responsibility. Despite the circumstances, you vow to improve whatever parts of you need improving and to find the next best company, person, or goal that is suited for the new you.

There are also times when denial can keep you from considering that you might be in the wrong business, or in the wrong place doing the wrong thing.

In 2016, I was paired with an African professional golfer in the annual Sunshine Tour Dimension Data Pro-Am. Richard (not his real name) was a nice man, kind and courteous to the amateurs like me during our rounds. He was twenty-eight years old and had been a pro for eight years. The winning pro that year was George Coetzee, who shot twenty-one strokes under par over the four rounds. Richard ended up twenty-four strokes over par (missing the cut after three rounds) and ended up dead last out of 168 pros.

After some early success in his career, Richard had reworked his swing, battled injuries, and was not making enough money on the tour to survive after paying entry, caddy and travel fees. We wanted to ask him if he thought he was in the wrong job and if he should consider being a teaching pro, course architect, and golf club designer—something within the field he loves but with a more realistic chance of success.

Playing competitively on the tour might not be his game. Though he was probably in the top 00.01 percent of all golfers in the world, unfortunately he was not performing well enough to be a truly top player in the professional money golf tours. I wanted to say something to him, so I gingerly asked him some questions about his life ambitions. I don't think he was in denial—he was probably working out with himself what to do next. Sometimes we ourselves have to come to that same conclusion, no matter how painful that is.

As you experience these common emotions after a failure, the key is not to allow yourself to become stuck in any of them, but to keep moving toward acceptance. Only then will you be ready to take the next steps toward your dream.

Failure Can Be an Excuse for Self-Destructive Behavior

After the five stages of grief, death is final. When you climb a dangerous mountain, things you're not ready for can have deathly consequences. When that happens, there is no bringing you back. When you "fail" at something, it does not have to be fatal, although sometimes it can be. Why? People fail to get all the way to the *determination* phase. They make a bad situation worse through drugs or alcohol, irrational or dangerous or careless behavior.

The alternative is something I call the Power of the Pivot. In basketball, once you have the ball, you can do a number of things: try to shoot the ball and make a basket, pass the ball to someone else, dribble, or pivot on one foot while you decide. If you move both feet at once without dribbling, it's called "traveling" and the ball is turned over to the other team.

Between the grieving and acceptance phases described above, you may want to look at pivoting—by moving to a new thing, person, or job that is adjacent to what you know and love. You could also decide to pass the ball to someone else, and they'll pass it back to you when you get closer to the basket or have a free shot.

What you don't want to do is make the situation worse by throwing the ball out of bounds, fouling someone, or taking a wild shot you have no chance of making. Especially at this difficult time, you need your wits to make an informed decision about necessary changes and your next journey.

So what do we learn from our "failures"?

- Resilience—that we're capable of overcoming our self-doubts and pressing on despite setbacks.

- Reflection—to know ourselves better, to see ourselves more clearly.

- Hope—the assurance that "the sun will come up tomorrow." No matter how things appear, they always seem better after a good night's sleep and when the sun is still shining through your window (though you might decide to close the curtains and go back to sleep).

- Perspective—the realization that we never see the whole picture until we step out of the frame. Some people do not learn and choose the same bad partner or job they're not suited for again and again. The goal is to learn something new from each failure and how to manage better next time. We have to rise above self-pity, self-loathing, and self-abuse. We need to honor the feelings of grief and give them meaning—by seeing the bigger picture as well as the frame.

What can we learn from success then?

- There will always be another "mountain" to climb, another summit to stand on. We can't become complacent—we have to look for the next big thing.

- If you've just won an Academy Award or had a record-setting sales year, you'll feel more pressure to overachieve next time. Marking the success with celebration is good and healthy. We can't rest on our laurels for too long, however, or assume that what worked for us one year will be equally effective and successful the next.

- We have an equal ability to propel ourselves forward or backward. We have to strive to get better, to improve and constantly reinvent ourselves, building on our past successes (and failures).

- What helped you reach your current pinnacle of success may not be enough to get you to the next level. We get older, our bones get brittle, our mind gets dimmer, and our wits become less sharp. We have to "live life on life's terms."

As you look back upon your life, both personally and professionally, you will see both successes and failures. Some of these events, of course, are cause for celebration, and others are cause for cringing. Both can be helpful as you learn from all your experiences and be better equipped for the next leap forward.

Questions to Help You Climb Higher

1. Check and recheck your goals, cause, or passion. Are they still what you want (for the right reasons)? Are you still committed to them? Are they realistic?

2. What stories are you telling yourself about your failure or success? What labels did you attach?

3. What has this revealed about yourself and what did you learn for your next attempt? Can you embrace a Higher Power for your higher purpose?

Strategies for Success

1. Honestly acknowledge your capabilities and failures. Allow yourself time to grieve and vow not to repeat the same mistakes again.

2. Don't make a bad situation worse. Remember the Power of the Pivot: no matter how bad the situation, you can pivot to something adjacent without sabotaging the rest of your life. Practice self-care and selflessness during the toughest times.

3. Enlist others to help you evaluate and challenge your beliefs, values, and persistence. Your ability to laugh at yourself and see the beauty in the world and others is most important, especially after experiencing failures and successes.

CHAPTER 12

MORE THAN SURVIVING

For Deborah Johnson, Tough Times and Tragedy Culminated in Helping Others Thrive

Some people make a big leap forward in their life based on careful planning and thorough preparation. They devise a bold strategy to launch a major transition, and when the time comes, they muster the courage to go for it.

Other people make leaps not according to any grand design but out of necessity—by responding to life's setbacks and challenges as best they can. Only by looking back can they see how far they've come and where they've arrived, even without intending to.

That is the case for Deborah Johnson, who has experienced more adversity than most people and who has responded with extraordinary resilience and perseverance. More than anything else, her inner strength propelled her forward, against the odds.

It's certain that Deborah's rough-and-tumble upbringing prepared her for the challenges she would later encounter. The fifth of ten children, she grew up in a close, loving, and colorful family. Raised in California's Bay Area, life as a child was filled with chores, rules, worship, squabbles, and mischief—or as she calls it, "beautiful chaos."

When Deborah was seventeen, her parents divorced after twenty-three years of marriage, with six kids still at home. As the oldest still around at that time, she unexpectedly and quickly left, as she says, "to avoid the responsibilities my older siblings experienced." So, still in her mid-teens, she found herself alone, renting a room, working five afternoons a week, and finishing her senior year at her third high school, intent on being the first in her family to graduate.

"When I think back, I shake my head in disbelief and wonder how I did it," she says. "But I quickly realize that my survival skills from a large family upbringing kicked in. I had to be scrappy, resourceful, and hard-working."

Shortly after graduation in July 1981, Deborah met a wonderful and loving man, seven years her senior; they fell in love, got to know each other well, and began making plans for a future together. A year into their relationship, however, they received devastating news: Deborah was diagnosed with an aggressive form of cancer.

Battle for Life

At age nineteen, Deborah's diagnosis was followed by major surgery, radiation, insertion of a Hickman catheter, and a year of chemotherapy. At first she was told her leg would be amputated from the knee. Fortunately, surgeons were able to save the leg but were forced to remove a significant amount of bone and tissue. They also performed a skin graft to move tissue from her buttocks to her leg.

All of this resulted in grueling physical therapy, significant scarring and disfigurement, and a permanent orthotic brace. She also lost her hair and had a few serious infections, which is common with therapy. As a daily reminder of her battle, she was surrounded by other oncology patients both young and old, many of whom did not survive.

Just to make a very rough situation even worse, as a result of such invasive treatments came the prognosis of infertility. "Anyone who has been diagnosed with a serious illness will understand how I felt—everything about the future was suddenly uncertain," she recalls. Nonetheless, Deborah was grateful to be alive and pushed herself to finish her chemotherapy in the hopes of being in remission.

Deborah's fight was complicated by the realities of being on her own, trying to work to make ends meet, and managing her health insurance along with treatments. Because of insurance and workers' comp restrictions, she arranged to work her full-time secretarial job for three weeks followed by a week off to receive chemotherapy at Presbyterian-Pacific Medical Center in San Francisco. She would then return to work on Monday morning, often feeling extremely nauseous.

Bred to be a fighter, Deborah battled through this horrendous season and eventually was deemed cancer-free. She married toward the end of her cancer treatments when she was twenty years old. The couple miraculously brought into the world a son and three daughters over the coming five years. Especially after her brush with death and excruciating treatments, Deborah felt extremely grateful to be a stay-at-home mom who was able savor moments with her family and friends.

"There is an indescribable appreciation about daily life after it has almost been taken away," she says. "All the simple pleasures meant so much to me. Of course, I experienced all the frustrations and aggravations that any mother goes through, but I knew how lucky I was to be alive. The doctors had told us we would never have children, but fortunately they were wrong."

Amid all the joys and preoccupations of managing a bustling family life, a recurring thought surfaced in Deborah's mind: She stressed the importance of higher education with her own kids, but was unable to earn her own college degree because of her illness and the succession of children who joined the family. To complicate the issue, Deborah regularly served on the PTA for her kids' schools, surrounded by women her age who were well-educated and corporate climbers. Her lack of college education had been a regret that gnawed at her for many years . . . but then that changed.

Better Late Than Never

Not knowing how to pursue a college education at age thirty-one, Deborah had built up daunting visions of what it took to earn a degree. Just how many years would it take while working and tending to the demands of a household? Was this a pipedream she would eventually abandon? Was it even worth it to try?

Undeterred by her doubts, and with years of encouragement and reassurance from her husband, Deborah drove to the local community college and met with a counselor. When the counselor outlined all the requirements and coursework, Deborah replied, "Is that it? I can do that!" So she dove into higher education with all the grit and gusto of someone given a second chance to pursue a dream.

129 —

To be sure, she needed that grit to get her through countless nights of cramming for tests and early mornings finishing term papers. While glad to finally be inching toward her degree, she realized it would be a long slog. Thankfully, she received motivation along the way in unexpected places.

Such encouragement occurred in 1997, when Deborah worked as a file clerk for a Menlo Park law office making $20 an hour while taking one community-college class per semester. Though grateful for the income, she admits it was mostly "grunt work" and not exactly challenging. On a particular afternoon, Deborah found herself on the floor, crawling under an attorney's desk to retrieve a file. Emerging, she looked up to see a newly hired female lawyer staring down at her. This attorney was young, attired in a tailored suit, with perfectly coifed hair and manicured nails.

When Deborah told her youngest daughter the story, her reply was, "Mom, that was your hell-no moment!" Deborah recalls with a chuckle. "I knew then that I was capable of more than filing—I had a lot more to offer the world. I thought, *If this young woman can become a lawyer and enjoy a prestigious career, then I can certainly do something meaningful with my life, too.* I knew I could do more and be more."

She redoubled her efforts and kept her end goal clearly in mind. Finally, at age 38 and after seven years at community college and two years at the university, she earned a bachelor's degree in health science. And Deborah didn't stop there. With much encouragement from her husband, she went back to college and earned a teaching credential in health and English.

At age forty, she landed her first high school teaching job at Foothill Middle College in Los Altos, earning $56,000 a year and providing insurance for her entire family, for which she was extremely proud! Beyond the financial rewards, she experienced an even bigger payoff—working with kids who had endured setbacks, fallen through the cracks, or otherwise were in danger of dropping out altogether.

"I was so proud of myself and loved working with the population of students I felt drawn to—at-risk youth, just like I had been. In fact, I stopped thinking of the kids as 'at-risk' and started referring to them as 'at-promise,' because they had great potential. They just needed support, guidance, and inspiration to help them reach that potential."

Amid those joyful, fulfilling times, another storm was brewing. This one close to home.

The Biggest Heartache of All

During Deborah's stable and satisfying years of the late 1990s and early 2000s, many people would have said that she had the "perfect family." Two parents in fulfilling careers, four well-adjusted kids who excelled at school, and a nice house in beautiful San Carlos . . . it was indeed a good life.

In 2004, however, Deborah's oldest child, Brian, then eighteen years old, began to display unusual behavior. Especially for Deborah, who worked with teenagers every day, signs began to appear that all was not right with her son. Brian had been universally known among friends and family as a sweet, curious, and loving kid. But that was changing as he became more sullen and angry. Experimenting more and more with marijuana, his moods became erratic. In time, he began making unusual statements, preoccupied with secrets of the universe, the double helix molecule, and religion.

131 —

Through a long journey of worrisome incidents, medical evaluations, and hospitalizations, Brian's physicians diagnosed him with schizophrenia. Over the coming year, Brian experienced three psychotic breaks, with delusional and paranoid episodes. More treatment, medication, and assistance followed—with family members and specialists doing all they could to help. Tragically, however, these interventions were not enough. On October 14, 2005, Brian took his own life, at age nineteen.

The shocking loss left Deborah, her family, and their entire community devastated and heartbroken. Deborah once again faced the question of how to move on amid heartache and sorrow.

Steps Forward

To allow herself time to heal and care for her family, Deborah left her teaching position and, after an extended time away, spent a year substitute teaching. She subbed often at a continuation school, Redwood High School, and immediately felt connected to the students. These were kids who, for a variety of reasons, were unsuccessful at their original schools and were struggling to graduate. Eventually, she was offered a full-time position at Redwood.

"I was still very fragile but accepted a low-key work-experience teaching position," she recalls. "It was a perfect pace for where I was emotionally at that time. Students transferring to a continuation school are fragile themselves, because of stress, family crises, poverty, or mental health challenges. They're just trying to navigate high school and life."

Because of her own challenging upbringing and the loss of her son, Deborah brought exceptional empathy and understanding to the students she worked with. At one point, the principal commented that she would make an excellent counselor and placed her in a temporary guidance counselor position. Three years later, at age forty-nine, Deborah earned her counseling credential and master's degree in education from San Jose State University.

"I've been a counselor for eight years, and I feel so grateful to have a career where I can use my life experiences—not only to connect, but to help guide, inform, and nurture young people. I am continually inspired and humbled by their kindness and perseverance in spite of the myriad challenges they face. It's heartwarming to see their progress, growth, and pride between the time they arrive and when they graduate."

Working with several hundred students each year, Deborah serves as a combination guidance counselor, academic coach, advocate, listening ear, encourager, and sometimes surrogate mom. She takes students on field trips to colleges and workplaces, giving them a vision for their future. Essentially, Deborah's work involves helping these young people take the next big leap in their lives by helping them find mentors, earn their diplomas, complete college applications, and obtain scholarships.

She is also heavily invested in giving these kids life experiences otherwise not available to them, such as excursions to the theater and museums, often paying out of her own pocket. Through countless hours spent with these teenagers, Deborah makes clear that she is concerned about their academic success but even more so about their emotional well-being.

For Deborah, it has been a long journey filled with many highs and lows. And she knows that life presents both opportunities and challenges all along the way. The latest came a few years ago when her marriage ended in divorce, bringing new difficulties to navigate. Given her history of resilience, Deborah is confident her future will continually open up to her in surprising and significant ways.

"None of my leaps forward were conscious or intentional—they just came out of my instinct for survival," she says. "But all of these experiences have brought me to where I am today, and I feel like I'm doing very meaningful work right now. Hopefully, that is an inspiration for other people to make a big change."

Though quick to deflect any excessive praise, Deborah has undoubtedly emerged not as a victim but a victor.

CHAPTER 13

EVERYBODY NEEDS A SHERPA
To Reach Your Peak, You'll Need Help
Along the Way

"To travel, to experience and learn: that is to live. I have climbed my mountain, but I must still live my life."
Tenzing Norgay

"I have never regarded myself as a hero, but Tenzing undoubtedly was."
Sir Edmund Hillary

I t happened on a Thursday morning on Mt. Everest.

I crouched on my hands and knees below the Hillary Step at around 28,500 feet, the last major climbing obstacle before the steady ascent to the summit of the world's tallest mountain. I was that close to reaching the top, but I couldn't breathe. I looked at my Sherpa, Lakpa, and motioned with my hands that I was suffocating.

My oxygen tank was either turned off or the mask was frozen, but suddenly I became totally focused on getting down the mountain and safely home. We had just gone up Mt. Everest's South Summit in an unexpected and fierce storm, with winds whipping at more than fifty miles per hour and temperatures without wind-chill sitting at -45c. At the top of the South Summit, we encountered a complete whiteout. The wind blew so furiously that my face and goggles were pelted with blowing snow, the icy pellets like projectiles against any exposed pores on my face.

At about this time—7:00 a.m.—almost every other climber had turned back due to the treacherous storm. I had just the remaining forty feet of the Hillary Step, which sits at an angle of forty-five to sixty degrees; after that, it was a mere five hundred meters to the summit. Yet, as I gasped for air, it might have been as far as the earth is from the moon.

I turned to Lakpa and mouthed, "What should we do?" He asked if my fingers and toes were okay, meaning not frozen. I nodded "yes." I can still see in every vivid detail how he then shrugged his shoulders as if to say, "It's your call."

I had no death wish and did not have "summit fever"— the sometimes irrational compulsion to reach the top. But I would have to make a decision whether to go on or to turn back, whether to risk our lives or to stand on the summit together.

A Sherpa's Value

What is a Sherpa? The dictionary's literal definition is "a member of a Himalayan people living on the borders of Nepal and Tibet, renowned for their skill in mountaineering."

That is certainly true, but there's a less formal usage of the term. We might also say that a Sherpa is someone in our lives—personally or professionally—who provides vital guidance, encouragement, wisdom, and direction on our journey. I strongly believe that we all need a Sherpa if we are going to reach our dreamed-of destinations.

The most famous Sherpa was Tenzing Norgay. On May 29, 1953, together with New Zealand climber Edmund Hillary, he was the first to summit Mount Everest. Norgay was named by *Time* magazine as one of the "100 Most Influential People of the Twentieth Century."

In 1953, Norgay took part in John Hunt's expedition, which was Hunt's seventh expedition to Everest. A member of the team was Hillary, who had a near fatality after falling into a crevasse. But he was saved from hitting the bottom by Norgay's prompt action in securing the rope using his ice axe. This led Hillary to consider him the climbing partner of choice for any future summit attempt.

Of Hunt's expedition, Norgay and Hillary were the first people to conclusively set their feet on the summit of Mt. Everest. After their descent, journalists persistently asked, "Which of the two men had the right to the glory of being the first one, and who was merely the second, the follower?"

Colonel Hunt, the expedition leader, declared, "They reached it together, as a team."

In recent years, Sherpas have died in avalanches in the Khumbu Icefall, a treacherous labyrinth of hidden crevasses, ice walls, and dangerous obstacles toward the base of Mt. Everest as you ascend from base camp. On April 18, 2014, a 14,000-ton block of ice slid down the southern face of Mt. Everest, killing sixteen people—thirteen of them Sherpas. It was the mountain's deadliest day, until just over a year later, when twenty-four died—half of them Sherpas—in the aftermath of the Nepalese earthquake that triggered fatal avalanches on the mountain.

These revered guides have long been undervalued as the true heroes of Everest. At times, they have fought with international climbers who did not show them the proper respect. At other times, they have been taken for granted by the media and parts of the climbing community, and have gone on strike to lobby for better treatment and fair pay. But for those who know their true value, the Sherpas are recognized as the unsung heroes on the mountain.

The Qualities of a Skilled Sherpa

Sherpas are compassionate, empathic, yet demanding leaders. They have immense perseverance, pride, and are extremely protective of their clients and the mountain. Sherpas help climbers learn from their mistakes. They will show you, for example, how to properly use your jumar (rope-climbing clamp) on a certain stretch of the mountain. Sherpas serve as coaches, therapists, and guides. They are also extremely spiritual. Sherpas are your "business partner"—they are invested in your success and their own. They do have a wicked sense of humor and are quite competitive--with them it's personal. And yes, they will help you carry your load.

Sherpas are not personal butlers. They are not robots—they are decidedly human with human emotions and feelings. Sherpas are not your yaks or your gofer. They will not carry you up the mountain, but they might save your life, or you theirs. They deserve respect and reverence from climbers, clients, and the public.

Not long before the deadly avalanche in 2014, Australian documentarian Jennifer Peedom arrived to make a film about the Sherpas. She had been on three Everest expeditions and had seen first-hand how their role in getting tourists to the top had been played down. Without a doubt, she knew there was a story to tell. But she couldn't have known that she would be there as news of the disaster rolled in.

After *Sherpa* was released in theatres, she acknowledged that it is not the film she intended to make. She argues, however, that the story that emerged is an essential one.

"They are a people moving toward self-determination, which is a very natural thing," says Peedom. "Sherpas are becoming better educated and going overseas. They're getting climbing credentials and coming back [to the western expedition leaders] and saying: 'I'm as good as you.' That puts pressure on the status quo."[1]

...

I first met my Sherpa, Lakpa, on the trek in from Lukla Airport to Everest Base Camp. There are daily flights from

139 —

Kathmandu to Lukla, which is the closest airport to Everest. Lakpa and I formed an easy bond, and I could feel a protective cocoon forming around me, both in a physical and metaphysical way.

If you met Lakpa on the street, you would instantly like him. He's tall, handsome, funny, charming, and of course, knowledgeable in all the mountain and spiritual ways. I took the time to get to know him on the ten-day trek to base camp. I learned where he was from, why he was there, and what made him unique as a person, rather than as my personal servant. A highlight was when we prayed together for safety and security from the mountain gods at our team's puja.

Lakpa was both patient and demanding—insisting that I practice safety above all else. He spent a good deal of time training me to self-arrest (a climber's ability to stop their own slide without the use of a rope or other belay system), and to employ self-care. I believe he also wanted to know that I could look after him in case of an emergency.

We were going to climb together, and though he would be *responsible* for me, I would be *accountable* for our success or failure. On our climbs through the dangerous Khumbu Icefall, we had a few mishaps, mostly all mine. One time I moved aside to let a faster group descend, and I stepped into a hidden crevasse. Luckily, the obstacle was not too deep and Lakpa pulled me out.

My most endearing memory of our time climbing together was getting ready to move out after a break. I'd get my equipment in order, ice axe at the ready, ropes secured, carabiner in place, and jumar on stand-by. And sometimes, if conditions were safe, I would insert earbuds and listen to music on my iPod. Lakpa would stand in front of me and double-check all my equipment for safety, and then, in what became a running joke, untwist the earbud cords and replace the earbuds in a touching kind of way.

A Sherpa of Your Own

In our own lives, in our own adventures, death-defying or not, we need our own Sherpas to check us and *check in* on us. We need them to help us make important adjustments, keep us going, and to laugh with us. They can give us strength and yet, at the same time, we can be there for *them*. You have to know you can't go it alone.

141 —

It is true that only you can get *yourself* to your goal, passion, or point of change. This might seem contradictory when we are talking about why we need Sherpas, but we alone are responsible for setting our goals and working toward them. Our Sherpas encourage us and shepherd us, but we alone have to make the commitment to do the training and hard work. You need your Sherpa, however, to help you and assist you.

Remember that your Sherpa is not your yak. In this mutually supportive relationship, you need to honor, recognize, and show gratitude toward your Sherpa along the way (and not just when you get to the summit). Very importantly, along with this respect there needs to be a willingness to debate, argue, and disagree, and ultimately decide together on the needed course of action or course correction.

To navigate the road toward your goals, you cannot hold back information, feelings, emotions, or health issues that can affect both you and your Sherpa. This person needs honest information so he or she can understand where you are in your journey and help you. Ultimately, you'll need to reciprocate by "paying it forward" and hopefully helping your Sherpa achieve their goals in the future.

How Do You Find Your Sherpa?

In order to find your Sherpa, you first need to be open to the "Sherpa-Climber" relationship—to allow someone else into your most intimate and darkest feelings and fears. You have to know where to look: in your network, among your friends, on a social site, or at your place of worship.

Think of a Sherpa as fulfilling three key roles:

1. Personal trainer

2. Therapist

3. Coach

Sherpas are different from mentors in that they are *personally invested in your goal, your passion, and your summit.* Think of them as your "business partner." Much like sponsors in AA, they cannot do the work for you and can't save you from yourself. They can, however, be there for you and tell you things others may not tell you, or give you the truth in a way you may not want to hear. In other words, mentors advise us while Sherpas are roped up to us. This is a critical difference.

As we have discussed, your relationship with your Sherpa must begin with respect for each other. Listen closely to that person. If you agree to do something, do it. Recognize the Sherpa during and after your success. Create outcome-based milestones and checkpoints for your expedition. Your journey will require you to have the right nutrition, fluids, equipment, gear and, most importantly, the right mind-set. Besides giving recognition, be there to help your Sherpa when they need it.

How Can You Become a Sherpa?

There are both formal and informal ways to become a Sherpa in someone else's life. Formally, you can volunteer your time and become a Big Brother or a Big Sister to someone in need. You might even come across people you don't know and "adopt" them, which is what happens in the wonderful film *The Pursuit of Happyness*. The film is about struggling single father Chris Gardner (played by Will Smith), and his fight to give a better life to his son, Christopher (played by Smith's real-life son, Jaden).

In the film, Smith's boss, Jay Twistle (played by Brian Howe), sees potential in the down-and-out Gardner and gives him a chance as a financial broker. Soon enough, Twistle's faith in Gardner is rewarded as he proves his worth to the company. I love this exchange between Gardner and Christopher:

> **Chris Gardner:** "Hey. Don't ever let somebody tell you … you can't do something. Not even me. All right?"

143 —

Christopher: "All right."

Chris Gardner: "You got a dream … You gotta protect it. People can't do somethin' themselves, they wanna tell you you can't do it. If you want somethin', go get it. Period."

Why are Sherpas so important in our lives? These are the men and women you can call on in the most difficult of times or situations, life-threatening or otherwise. These are the folks who are there for you in the middle of the night when you need someone to talk to you and give you honest advice. They are your advocates—they want what you want.

Sherpas can keep you safe, but they can't always save you. This is where the (mountaineering term) self-arrest comes in. They're like your blood brothers or sisters who are in tune with your dreams, passions, and fears. Like any good partnership, it's a two-way street of looking after them in the same way and being there for them.

• • •

After Lakpa shrugged his shoulders at me below the Hillary Step, I knew *the decision was mine but the outcome was ours.* He was checking in on me for safety and looking at my face for clues that I was mentally prepared not just for the summit, but also for the descent back to safety.

When we started up the South Col that evening, a half moon was out and the skies were clear. It was still and quiet, with just our crampons biting into the ice and snow, headlamps ahead to guide us as we ascended, alone with our thoughts. Then the storm hit, with 50-mile-per-hour winds and temperatures (with wind-chill) that dropped to more than -50c. The white-out was upon us, and we knew we were in trouble. To make matters even more dire, my oxygen ran out. At that moment, I thought about all my friends and family—they were with me in this critical moment and the rest of the way.

Shortly after running out of oxygen, Lakpa and I were there, standing at the foot of the Hillary Step. When that moment of truth came and we had to decide to go on or turn back, I knew I wanted to live; I wanted to see what the universe had to offer. That is when Lakpa gave me the choice—after measuring me, studying me, to see if I was fit to continue. If he had said we should turn back, I would have. Since he was my Sherpa, I trusted him fully. Instead, he left it up to me.

145 —

I decided we should push on. We cleared the Hillary Step and navigated the last five hundred meters toward the summit. The final ascent is up a narrow spine of mountain, with an eight-thousand-foot drop to Nepal on one side and a nine-thousand-foot drop to Tibet on the other. All I could do was make sure every step mattered and keep going forward.

Suddenly, there it was . . . the top. It looked like a mirage in the whiteness. We took our last steps together and clipped in at the highest point on the planet. We hugged each other, and it was surreal. I had summited without oxygen.

Honestly, I wanted to do a few things then: take some pictures, eat some food, drink some water, get some oxygen, fly the flags I'd brought (and take a pee). But Lakpa wanted to make sure we respected and honored the mountain (called Sagarmāthā in the local language). Lakpa and I spent a few minutes in prayer and then offered some donations and candy to the mountain before we made sure we were prepared for the dangerous descent. Any true celebrations would have to wait until we had returned to safety.

The following year Lakpa would accompany my friend and fellow climber, Sondra, from Denali, Alaska, on her expedition up Everest. Going up the Lhotse Face, above 23,000 feet, Lakpa was hit by a rock below his helmet and had to be helicoptered out. Sondra eventually summited with another Sherpa. In 2016, five years after our adventure, Lakpa guided my old climbing partner, Paula, to the top. We've remained in contact through all these years, and we each sign off our emails with the words, "Your Lifelong Friend."

In your journey up your mountain, either metaphorical or actual, you need a "Lakpa" who can guide, encourage, and safeguard you. Don't fall into the trap of thinking you can do it alone. Finding a Sherpa can make all the difference between success and failure for your quest.

Questions to Help You Climb Higher

1. Do you want a Sherpa? Are you prepared to commit to yourself and to him or her?

2. Are you willing to invest the time to be one and to have one? What life changes might you need to make to create the time and energy for a Sherpa relationship?

3. Who can you be a guide or Sherpa for? Think of people you know who would benefit from this arrangement, and broach the idea of being "roped up" together.

Strategies for Success

Knowing how vital the Sherpa relationship is, here are ideas for developing one successfully:

1. Know the difference between roles. You'll need a navigator (guide or mentor), a Sherpa (responsible and hands-on) and, porters; but ultimately, you are accountable. The navigator can show you where to go, the Sherpa can intimately support you on the way, and the porter can help you carry your load when you need a little help. Recognize, acknowledge, and appreciate your crew—some of your crew will be there just "for a season, for a reason," while others will remain with you throughout your life.

2. Give of yourself and your most precious commodity—your time. Be there for your crew in their hardest moments on the journey, and celebrate in their successes. Be present in their lives.

3. ALOHA. In the movie The *Fundamentals of Caring*, Paul Rudd plays a new caregiver and learns about and tries to practice the acronym ALOHA: Ask, Listen, Offer, Help, and Ask Again. What a fantastic reminder to keep in mind when being a Sherpa.

We are motivated by, and learn from, people who have gone before us. They pass along their wisdom and share their experiences. For every big goal we set out to achieve and big change we seek to make, we will benefit from Sherpas who come in many forms. Although you have to do the climbing yourself, they can help you carry your load, set the ropes, and provide counsel. You will have to be able to self-arrest, self-soothe, and self-help, for your own self-achievement—but you can do it with another and stand on the mountain as a team.

Looking into the sky, what would I face?
Would I only try, or just try to keep pace
The icefall it rose and tumbled and fell
As if in a pose, that looked all pell-mell

Snow and ice, devoid of all life
Challenging my insides, cutting me like a knife
What would I face, at the Hillary Step?
When I couldn't keep pace, where others had crept

Like a climber who knows, his worst fears are close
The bodies whose souls, are there and in pose
How do you know, when your dreams can come true?
From our strength that was so, from others that we
knew

I saw high above, the peak that stood tall
All surrounded by love, and my worries were small
When I saw her shining face, through the clouds that
broke free
I knew I had to say grace, and be who I could be

I took one step forward, and kept my mind free
Tried not to go backward, and see what I could see
And then it was my duty, I stood on her top
And worshiped her beauty, not intending to stop

Mitch Lewis, *Ode To Everest*
June 2012

CHAPTER 14

A MODERN-DAY "GREEK LEGEND"

Alf Field Knows a Thing or Two about Finishing What He Starts

Anyone who completes just one marathon these days—officially, a distance of 26.21 miles—can never be accused of lacking perseverance or determination. The race is a grueling test of physical, mental, and emotional stamina.

But then, what words are left to adequately describe someone who has run 110 of them—a total of 2,884 miles—all between the age of forty and sixty-three? Tenacious? Stubborn? Driven? The problem intensifies when you learn that after injuring his knee in a freak accident in 2003—effectively ending his running career—this man got back in the saddle to participate in a four-day, three-hundred-mile bicycle race from London to Paris.

Emboldened by that, Alf Field has since completed seven triathlons. That's a brutal combination of endurance races in biking, swimming, and running (in his case, he walked the run leg of each event). In 2016, at age seventy-six, he was preparing for his eighth triathlon when he was temporarily sidelined by the only force that seemed capable of slowing him down: a bout with aggressive prostate cancer.

"A triathlon this year is out of the question," Alf said just before undergoing surgery, which turned out to be a success. "Next year is another story."

Perhaps Alf is actually the reincarnation of Pheidippides, the Greek soldier who, according to legend, ran twenty-two miles from the blood-soaked battlefields of Marathon to Athens to announce the defeat of the Persian army—after fighting in the battle himself. The man is said to have run the whole distance without resting.

Upon arrival Pheidippides shouted, "We have won!"—then promptly dropped dead. That's the kind of heroic achievement the founders of the modern Olympic Games sought to commemorate when the marathon race was established in 1898. It's a standard that Alf Field seems to have taken to heart . . . only stopping short of perishing after each race.

As to what words best describe such a life, Alf himself acknowledges the role of the "alpha male personality." With that personality type, he began by running in a fourteen-kilometer race, and advanced from there.

"If you've done ten miles, you want to be able to do a half-marathon," he says. "If you've done a half-marathon, you want to be able to do a marathon, then a double marathon. Then all the time you're thinking, *I need to improve my times*, so it's constant self-imposed pressure."

As it happens, history does hold some insight into the origin of such determination—but not that of the Greeks. To better understand what drives Alf to epic feats of endurance, you need look no further than his own family history in his native land of South Africa.

153 —

Born to Make a Mark

Alf Field came into the world in 1940 on the family farm at Driefontein, in South Africa. His father was away at the time with the 2nd South African Brigade fighting in North Africa against the legendary "Desert Fox"—German Field Marshal Erwin Rommel. After Rommel's defeat at El Alamein in late 1942, the elder Field was finally sent home again.

When Alf was eight years old, doctors told his mother his heart had been severely damaged by rheumatic fever—and participation in sports was out of the question. Sitting on the sidelines while the other boys played often made him a target of ridicule. The other kids called him a wimp and a coward.

"It's not a good idea to call me a wimp today!" he quips.

One day the rugby team was short a player and asked Alf to join in. He recalls thinking if he were going to die, he'd rather it come as a result of doing something he loved. He agreed, and the team found him a "wet, smelly" shirt that had been worn in a previous game, but could find no boots to fit him. A lack of shoes didn't prevent him from scoring the winning try that day—and becoming a permanent member of the team.

On hearing the news, his mother dragged him straight to the doctor, who could no longer hear the "heart murmur" that had caused such alarm just five years earlier.

The farm where Alf grew up was within sight of a broad ancestral valley in the Witteberg mountain range known as Moolmanshoek. It derives its name from the first settlers to make a home there, the Moolman family—Alf's family. The Moolmans arrived in 1829, among the "Voortrekkers"— Boer farming families who migrated east from Cape Town to escape British colonial rule. Alf's grandfather subsequently fought in the Boer War against Great Britain, spending much of the conflict in a British prisoner of war camp.

Sir Arthur Conan Doyle famously wrote that history had formed the Boers into "one of the most rugged, virile, unconquerable races ever seen upon Earth"—owing to their skill and ferocity as warriors, huntsmen, and horsemen. "Put a finer temper upon their military qualities by a dour fatalistic Old Testament religion and an ardent and consuming patriotism," he added. "Combine all these qualities and all these impulses in one individual, and you have the modern

Boer—the most formidable antagonist who ever crossed the path of Imperial Britain."

Move forward through time, and it seems having Boer blood in your veins can still make you exactly the kind of person capable of playing rugby with no shoes—and taking up running after age forty, never looking back.

A Migration of Their Own

Alf has more than extraordinary determination in common with his ancestors. In 1979, he and his wife, Rosanne, became modern-day Voortrekkers, leaving behind their home and successful business in South Africa to escape political and social conditions there.

"Living in South Africa during the apartheid era created a situation where we felt obliged to try and do something about it," Alf recalls. "I got involved in politics, but that didn't work too well. After that, I believed the only option was to leave the country and go somewhere else to start a new life."

With four kids under age eleven to care for, the decision proved to be difficult. In South Africa, Alf said, the family employed two maids to help care for the kids. Elsewhere there would be "no such luxury," but their deep conviction that something was terribly wrong with apartheid made that a risk worth taking.

The Fields considered all options, including emigrating to the United States. A client there urged them to consider Los Angeles as a destination, and even went so far as to arrange a meeting with a dozen wealthy "oil widows" in need of Alf's expertise in financial management.

"But in the end, we decided Americans drive on the wrong side of the road and play the wrong sports," he says. "The culture shock would have been much more difficult, especially for the kids. They played cricket and rugby and understood those things."

That made Australia the obvious choice. With a solid income from investments back in their native country, the family set out for Sydney to make a new life. That's when Alf seized the opportunity to change more than his home and occupation. He went to work on himself.

"When I arrived in Australia, I was overweight and approaching forty. I thought, *I've got to make a change and start taking care of myself physically.* That's when I took up running, but it wasn't easy because I weighed so much. With my first run while trying to get in shape, I just tried to make it around the block, and my family almost had to call an ambulance for me."

But he kept at it—and quickly dropped fifty pounds. Thanks to encouragement from friends, Alf soon found a more tangible motivation for his persistence—an invitation to participate in the annual City to Surf "fun run" covering fourteen kilometers from Sydney Town Hall to Bondi Beach.

"I didn't know how I was going to run a 14K," Alf recalls. "So I got Rosanne to take me out in the car one day. I told her, 'We're going to drive out into the national park. Every

5K, we'll drop a bottle of water. When we reach 15K, you'll drop me and go home. Then I'll run home.'"

And that's what he did. In the process, he proved to himself that distance running wasn't an impossible dream. Today, after hundreds of miles of running, biking, and swimming, he points to that day with the water bottles as the genesis of his remarkable athletic career.

"When I found I could do that, I became comfortable with the idea," he says. "The sense of achievement when I did that first City to Surf run was fantastic."

A Freak Accident and a New Challenge

Twenty-three years later, Alf's running career came to an end when he stepped off a curb to make way for someone to pass by—and tore the meniscus in his knee. He was sixty-three years old. That might not have been the end if he'd heeded a doctor's advice and undergone immediate orthoscopic surgery to repair the damage. Instead, he went through with plans to head south the following February—and run in the Antarctica Marathon.

"I did that marathon with a dodgy knee," he admits. "That, I'm afraid, was the end of my running career, really. My body eventually told me, 'That's it. Better find something else to do.'"

Not one to spend time on the sideline willingly—or let a challenge go unanswered—Alf soon found a replacement activity: bicycling. A close friend happened to be training for an endurance bicycle race from London to Paris and invited

Alf to join him. The man was more than a decade older than Alf.

"I thought, *Well, if he can do it at seventy-five and I'm ten years younger, I don't see why I can't do it. It was only three hundred miles.*"

Riding into Paris at the end of that trip reminded him of completing the City to Surf years earlier—and the sense of possibility he'd lost after his injury returned. Armed with a renewed determination, he looked for the next big challenge and quickly found it: the Noosa Triathlon in the Australian state of Queensland. Since he could do no more than walk the 10K run portion of the race, Alf came in dead last. He crossed the finish line long after the support staff had begun cleaning up and dismantling the watering stations.

"I was in tears as I finished," he says. "People wanted to have their photos taken with me. Talk about a huge buzz of satisfaction and excitement. This feeling of accomplishment becomes addictive, and I have now done seven Noosa Triathlons."

"Give It a Go"

Today, Alf is focused on recovering his health after prostate surgery—with a promise to take is slow for a while. "For once, I'm prepared to listen to advice," he says.

Alf offers simple guidance to anyone who might feel stuck in life and facing seemingly overwhelming obstacles.

"Don't be daunted by any challenge, no matter how difficult it may seem," he says. "Invariably there are ways to do it, you just have to sort them out and plan for them and give it a go. Find a challenge that seems impossible and give it a go."

CHAPTER 15

THERE WILL BE BLOOD, SWEAT, AND TEARS

Any Journey Worth Taking Is Going to Require Grit and Determination

"Both tears and sweat are salty, but they render a different result. Tears will get you sympathy; sweat will get you change."
Jesse Jackson

"Don't sweat the petty things and don't pet the sweaty things."
George Carlin

The expression "blood, sweat, and tears" is often said to have been coined by Sir Winston Churchill. He spoke these words in his famous 1940 speech when he warned the British people of the hardships to come in World War II, saying, "I have nothing to offer but blood, toil, tears and sweat." But it wasn't actually Churchill who coined this phrase; the roots of the expression have a Christian historical source.

The first occurrence of the expression found in print is in *Sermons on Various Subjects* by Christmas Evans (apropos name), translated from the Welsh by J. Davis in 1837: "Christ the High Priest of our profession, when he laid down his life for us on Calvary, was bathed in his own blood, sweat, and tears."[1]

Al Kooper picked up on the phrase as the name for his new jazz-rock band in 1967, *Blood, Sweat and Tears*, which went on to record such chart-topping hits as "You Make Me So Very Happy" and "Spinning Wheel." Kooper could hardly have known how apt a choice his band name would become. The band has gone through more disagreements, firings, and artistic changes than most, with at least a hundred and forty musicians having been members at some point.

All of this brings us to you: When you have to deal with setbacks, delays, heartbreaks, and pain on your journey toward achieving your passion, you will truly find out how strong you are. You'll test your mettle when you have to dig deep and find your inner strength. Think of it this way: *Blood* is the fight, *Sweat* is the work, and *Tears* are the emotions. Dedication to our cause and our ability to overcome the obstacles the universe throws at us comes from our blood, sweat, and tears.

I learned this firsthand through some of my mountain-climbing lessons, the most vivid being my trek up Denali (aka Mt. McKinley). During my climb up North America's highest peak, my fellow climbers and I had to carry sixty pounds in our packs, as well as pull our own sleds of equal weight. This was not much less than the hundred and thirty pounds I weighed at the time. On some of the steepest sections and the hardest carries, I found myself counting steps just to distract my mind, telling myself, *One step at a time. One more step.*

As a marathon and ultra-marathon runner, I have had this experience many times. I have wanted to give up on numerous occasions, especially when I started to dwell on how many miles were left in a particular race. It really was "mind over matter," when just carrying on and pushing through the pain was the best I could do—all the while trying to keep the end goal in mind.

163 —

The Finish Line Matters Most

Just like when racing or climbing a mountain, the physical exertion to meet your goals might be easy at first. Such "beginner's success" sometimes fools us into thinking that our process is going to be a piece of cake. But we need to be aware that hardships lie ahead, for which we may be unprepared. There's an old saying that "the race is not won at the beginning but at the end." How true. If we know in advance that our path forward will include obstacles—and sometimes debris—such awareness can help us to stay focused on our objectives. Some personalities actually thrive on pushing through the pain and love the challenge when it happens, even when the problem is unforeseen and daunting.

During such times of adversity, this is where your Sherpa and team can offer you the help you need. So many times in a race or on the trail, during the darkest moments a stranger or friend would give me words of encouragement. At those times, a small pat on the back felt like a big shot of adrenaline and gave me the courage to persevere.

We have to be prepared to stick with our commitment and follow through with our plans. We also have to be ready for the sacrifices that our passion will require. You cannot get something without giving something up. Just like Mick Jagger sang, "You can't always get what you want, but sometimes you get what you need." You do have to sacrifice some things in your life to make room for your passion; you really can't have it all. You have to be willing to say no—for a while—to things you desire in order to achieve your ultimate goal.

The cost of the climbs and gear meant I had to forgo a new roof for the house or trading in my old car for a few years. I had to give up time with my family and friends to spend long hours training. I had to say no to certain foods and drinks to get into the best possible shape.

But in the end, it was all worth it, like it will be for you. (An important caveat here: You will need to pay back, as best you can, the time lost with your family and loved ones. While it is true that we can't get the time back, we can vow not to overlook those who are most important to us.)

One more thing we can certainly do is laugh and remind ourselves that the pain and sacrifice will all make for a great story later on. The hardest part is to laugh at our crazy idea—and the situation—while in the moment. We can also decide if we can handle the situation better next time. I've been known (very rarely) to throw a golf club after a bad shot.

Afterward, not only do I feel bad, but I can't understand how I thought this would help me! Not only do I embarrass myself, but I cause a distraction for my golf partners. When the club has actually been damaged, I have to tell myself my own advice: Don't make a bad situation worse! Sometimes it's hard to take our own advice.

It's also true that we can't make up time, distance, or scores all at once. We can't run a two-minute mile or hit a hole-in-one on a 555-yard par five. We can only take it a step at a time, a shot at a time. We need to shake off whatever happened before and move on to what we can control in the present moment.

The Concept of Blood, Sweat, and Tears

Everyone breathes faster and deeper (hyperventilates) at high altitude—it is necessary to survive. The function of the lungs is to expose blood to fresh air, and breathing faster increases the flow of fresh air past the blood. The oxygen present in inhaled air diffuses into the blood in the lungs.

Blood has a massive capacity to dissolve oxygen—much more oxygen can dissolve in blood than can dissolve in the same amount of water. This is because blood contains haemoglobin, a specialized protein that binds to oxygen in the lungs so the oxygen can be transported to the rest of the body. The amount of haemoglobin in blood increases at high altitude.

This is one of the best-known features of acclimatization (acclimation) to high altitude. Increasing the amount of haemoglobin in the blood increases the amount of oxygen that can be carried. The same is true in our analogy: We are, in effect, acclimatizing during our "climb" toward our passion or goals.

Blood is what appears when you are "bloodied" in a fight. As a figure of speech, we try to "stop the bleeding" when we are in a bad situation at work or in life. Sometimes we are haemorrhaging (hurting badly, going through a tough time), and we have to take drastic action to stay alive and to stay in the fight. We might also get metaphoric blood blisters on our feet from the long journey; they're painful, but not life threatening, and we might just need a form of "different shoes" to continue on.

Perspiration is the production of fluids secreted by the sweat glands in the skin of mammals. In humans, sweating is primarily a means of thermoregulation, which is achieved by the water-rich secretion of the eccrine glands. Maximum sweat rates of an adult can be up to 2–4 liters per hour or 10–14 liters per day! (Who knew?) Sweat is how our body cools itself down. Without it, we would overheat—it literally acts as our radiator.

Thomas Edison once famously said, "Genius is 1 percent inspiration, 99 percent perspiration." The point is that sweating is a biological response, whereas giving of our own sweat is necessary to achieve our goals.

Biologists note that "tearing . . . is the secretion of tears, which often serves to clean and lubricate the eyes in response to an irritation of the eyes." But the truth is that crying happens from strong emotions, such as sorrow, elation, love, awe or pleasure.

We cry when we're happy, frustrated, angry, depressed, or sad. We shed tears over a lost loved one or a lost goal. We cry when we lose faith and think we can't go on. We also shed tears of joy and elation. This is why we see so many athletes or actors cry when they receive a trophy.

If you were overwhelmed with joy, would you hide a smile? So if you're sad, why wouldn't you cry? Why wouldn't you give yourself the right to be sad or mad? People who ignore sadness cheat themselves out of an important facet of life. Sadness, or crying, isn't a sign of weakness, it's a sign that you're a human being and have feelings.

Much like a spit valve releases saliva from a trumpet, your tear ducts release stress, anxiety, grief, and frustration from your brain and body. It is soul cleansing, almost acting as a drain for the build-up of negative emotions that result from stress. The healing properties of tears aren't just restricted to sad tears, but happy tears as well. In either case, you're dealing with extreme emotion.

In your own journey, you are going to have many times when you feel like crying or actually do. It's a good thing. Allowing extreme emotion to back up and stay in the body can be dangerous both physically and mentally. Crying tears of happiness or sadness are indeed necessary.

I promise you that all the blood, sweat, and tears will all be worth it. You will be tested in ways you never thought possible. You will overcome things that you never dreamt you were capable of. You will achieve things that were worth the toll because of where it will take you. And, perhaps most importantly, you will learn more from how you dealt with storms than if all you had ever encountered were blue skies and sunshine. Setbacks and letdowns are part of any significant endeavor. Dealing with disappointments—and maybe even disasters—is an important element for success.

Perseverance, Then Pay-Off

Like everyone else who has ever walked the planet, I've had my share of failures, setbacks, disasters, pain, and suffering. I overcame my height disadvantage to make my high school basketball team (even if it was the C squad). I lost my first telesales job at age sixteen because my boss thought I was spying for a competing company (which I wasn't). I ended up at AT&T because of this.

I was on-point for many network cutovers during my technician days, transforming the network from analog to digital. One time, I brought down the network in parts of Los Angeles due to one missed connection. I ended up in a better and more senior role because of—or in spite of—my error.

We had wireless equipment component shortages when I was the managing director in Indonesia, with angry customers complaining to our CEO during his visit to Jakarta. This set the stage for me to play a key role in the network restoration after the 2004 earthquake and tsunami.

There is a famous business book called *First 90 Days* by Michael Watkins that outlines strategies for new leaders in organizations. The hiring manager at Microsoft gave me a copy of the book before I started. It's filled with scary tales of failure and encouraging stories of success. But in the end, the book was no help at Microsoft when my boss, who hired me, left after forty-five days. Thankfully, this difficult transition ultimately led to a bigger and better position for me at Juniper Networks (one of the IT/telecom network leaders as a key competitor to Cisco).

In all of these endeavors and situations, I went through the stages of grief but somehow found strength to move to acceptance and determination. My breakthroughs did not come, however, without first shedding tears over injustice, bad luck, circumstances beyond my control, or my own bad moves.

In contrast, I cried tears of happiness on finding love, intimacy, and romance. These tears often came with the realization after lost loves taught me that there was something better, though I did not know it at the time. I cried tears of joy over holding my first grandchild; it made up for all the times that my son would frustrate me during his teenage years.

Seeing my wife, Michelle, cry in the rain after she finished her first marathon in Hawaii made me appreciate another person's achievement. My frozen tears of accomplishment

169 —

while standing on the summit of Everest made the years of training and sacrifice all worthwhile.

Words of encouragement from my friends, colleagues, guides, and Sherpas have surely helped me. I have always tried to call on my "crew" when in need and have always tried to keep my "eyes on the prize." Having patience, staying the course, and admitting my failures publicly and privately helped me the next time a similar situation came about.

I tried to take care of myself after these setbacks. I would resolve to eat better, exercise, practice mindfulness, and appreciate the natural beauty of our world. I would try to practice "fast-forgetfulness" and work to compartmentalize and file away the setbacks—and to remember the lessons learned. Having said this, it was not always a straight line, and saying it was never the same as actually doing it.

As well, I've worked hard on forgiveness, which is an important concept. I strive to let people off the hook as I would want them to do with me. To help me stay on track, I developed and used the concept of **DRIVE**:

> **Disappointment**. Acknowledge the original issue and the feelings it caused within you. Then move on to ...

> **Resolve**. Learn from the failure or shortcoming and resolve not to make the same mistake again. And then ...

> **Inquiry**. Just as in an accident investigation, hold your own inquiry; this can be short so that you

fortify your . . .

Values. These are what keep you persevering and getting past obstacles so you can move to the phase of . . .

Execution. This is the process of getting this behind you and doing something differently to change.

Find your own acronym, mantra, or catchphrase—whatever works for you—to help you in your wondrous journey of self-discovery as you move toward your personal passion.

Questions to Help You Climb Higher

1. How committed are you to your goal or passion? Are you mentally prepared to go through the desert—to feel the pain, the burn, and to power through?

2. How many hours are you prepared to invest, and what are you willing to sacrifice, to achieve your goal? Are you self-aware of your inherent weaknesses, have the ability to change your routines, and put in the training to change and improve?

3. Have you visualized what success will look like? In effect, have you written your "acceptance speech" for when you receive your first Academy Award? Have you written a letter from the future—one that documents where you'll be, what you've visualized, what you want the universe to give you?

Strategies for Success

How do you make perseverance pay off? Start with these ideas:

1. Sometimes you have to slow down to speed up. Take one small step at a time rather than trying to conquer the whole thing at once. It's like the old saying, "How do you eat an elephant? One bite at a time." (But please do not eat elephants.)

2. Stay the course. Keep your eyes on the prize and stay focused. Climb at the right trajectory. Hang on during the toughest times and know things will get better, but sometimes they get worse first. Stay in the right direction, learn to recover, and "get back on your bike." Practice self-care, just like the airline instructions: "Secure your own mask first before you help others."

3. Call on your crew. Enlist the help of family, friends, colleagues, and children—those who are there for life as well as those who temporarily come alongside for a specific purpose.

CHAPTER 16

A WAY TO GIVE BACK

Karen McDaniels Found Post-Career Purpose Among the World's Poorest People

Karen McDaniels could be spending all her time traveling or lounging on an idyllic beach somewhere—and no one would blame her. She could be perfecting her tennis backhand or lowering her golf handicap or touring the wineries of Tuscany. She could be anywhere, doing anything. After more than four decades in the high-stress world of corporate business—with a gold watch from multinational conglomerate 3M to show for it—she's earned the right to a little retirement R&R.

But at this point in her life, taking the easy way is not Karen's style.

Instead, she's committed her heart and time and labor to the last place on earth you would expect to find a successful American businesswoman: Cirendeu, an open garbage dump in Jakarta, Indonesia. To be more precise, she has devoted her retirement to the one hundred-plus families who live and work there—just a few of the estimated five hundred thousand "trash pickers" in Jakarta.

"It had always been about me and my plan," Karen says, looking back on her career in business. "How much money do I need to retire, and how am I going to get it? How am I going to be successful? How can I move up the ladder? Thankfully, I achieved the level of success I'd aimed for—but then found a way to use the gifts I've been given to help those not blessed with many such gifts."

Not Quite Right

When it comes to employment history, Karen is a rarity of loyalty and longevity these days. She went to work at age sixteen and retired at fifty-eight—but in all those years she held only three jobs. The last of them—which was hers for more than twenty-five years—was a challenging and rewarding relationship with a company she loved: 3M. The corporation employs nearly ninety thousand people in sixty-seven countries—and produces more than fifty thousand products, from adhesives to telecommunications systems.

She laughs when asked what her job description was upon retirement. "I honestly don't know, I did so many things over the years—sales, marketing, business development, mentoring, training. I used to collect all my different business cards, but I gave that up."

Whatever her role, she genuinely enjoyed the work and was never bored. Not only was her work financially rewarding, but it also gave her a sense of purpose and creative stimulation.

"I would sit in a lot of meetings, but they weren't boring meetings at all," she recalls. "They were the kind where you could see what the future of the company was going to be. They were exciting."

Even so, near the end of her career—upon returning to the U.S. after many years in Southeast Asia—she admits that "everything seemed not quite right" in her life.

"I felt off center," she admits. "I think it had to do with the fact that for years I'd been working in different cultures and crossing time zones and being so busy that I didn't really take time for me. I would get on an airplane, and that became time to work, or to read reports or examine spreadsheets. That was me for years and years."

The beginning of a solution presented itself when she moved to Austin, Texas, and a friend recommended she give yoga a try. She did, and the ancient spiritual practice was an instantaneous fit. Quite simply, she says, on the yoga mat she found her "soul." Before long, Karen knew she had to learn more about yoga than a few minutes of class a week could deliver, so she enrolled in a school to become a yoga instructor herself.

"Going to school was about more than learning to be a teacher," she says. "It was about understanding the yogic tradition and the Hindu tradition at a deep level. Yoga is not separate from your life, it *is* your life."

Karen says yoga and a vegan diet have combined to give her as much energy now as she had as a thirty-year-old. Making those changes in her lifestyle, along with completing Tony Robbins' personal development program Mastery University, added up to a new lease on life—and a new direction.

A Place in the World

Karen's spiritual journey has involved learning to recognize the magical moments when "spirits" connect, and to understand what she's meant to do when that occurs. Though she didn't know it at the time, her life was about to change—and her purpose to become clearer—the day she met an impassioned Indonesian woman named Retno Hapsari.

The two women met initially when Karen became interested in craft goods made from recycled garbage collected by so-called "trash pickers" in Indonesia. These are multigenerational families who sort through rubbish on the streets and in the dumps of Jakarta in order to eek out a meager living. Karen had become aware of the plight of such people when living in Jakarta years earlier.

Among the many thousands of trash pickers in Jakarta, the men of the family rise early each day to comb through mounds of garbage for anything that will fetch a price from recycling companies. Women then sort and clean the haul, which typically brings in around $5 a day. Children born into trash picker families join the work at an early age. Trash pickers lack adequate housing, nutrition, sanitary water, and access to health care and education.

"They live in a garbage dump," Karen says. "There's smoke in the air, and the water they drink is unclean. Many people contract tuberculosis. The conditions are truly deplorable."

Karen's interactions with Hapsari initially centered on the business side of selling up-cycled products to benefit the trash pickers—a mission Hapsari pursues in her role as general manager of the Indonesian nonprofit organization XSProject. But Karen quickly realized there was more to the woman's goals than that.

"When I finally met Retno in person, I saw that her operation was very different from what I thought it was," McDaniels recalls. "I thought she was just making a product to sell to help the trash pickers. But her heart was in a completely different place. More than anything, she wanted to stop the children from picking trash. The problem was, she didn't know how to do it."

That's where Karen's decades of business experience came in—with skills that included mentoring, training, business development, and marketing. Over time it became clear that what Hapsari and others like her lacked was someone to show them how to achieve their goals.

"Indonesia was under dictatorship for more than thirty years," Karen says. "There was no rule of law and lots of corruption. People were pretty much told where to go, what to do, and how to think. So a lot of what I do now is mentoring. I show people how to realize the things they dream about."

That advice includes how to structure a non-profit organization, raise and handle money, network and mobilize necessary resources, and translate big dreams and ambitious goals into successful action. Under Karen's guidance, XSProject has grown to include: more than one hundred children in the XSEducation school program; vocational training for young men and women to help them escape trash picking; access to free health care through a cooperative relationship with a Jakarta hospital; and a partnership with the Cilandak Rotary Club International to distribute water filtration systems to trash picker families. In August 2015 alone, XSProject handed out seventy filters, leading to a measurable reduction in the health-related effects of drinking contaminated water.

These endeavors are paid for, in part, because XSProject buys items from the trash pickers for which a recycling market does not otherwise exist, things that are then incorporated into a variety of craft items such as wallets, tote bags, and computer covers. Product sales fund the business operations of XSProject, paying the expenses of running the workshop and the wages of employees who work in the trash picker community.

Although sales help defray costs, much of the organization's financial support is due to Karen's fundraising efforts and the generous donor base cultivated over the years. In fact, about 80 percent of Karen's work involves fundraising at speaking engagements, trade shows, and other events.

"I want to see no more trash pickers anywhere," says Karen. "Until then, I want to see every trash picker's child have an education. That will make the world a much better place."

Every Day a New Adventure

When Karen McDaniels retired, she knew only one thing for sure: She had no intention of "sitting down and doing nothing."

Instead, she has followed her intuition and the nudging of kindred spirits with whom she has connected along the way. Because of that, she's made a real difference in the lives of some of the world's poorest people—and she has no plans to stop anytime soon.

"I'll keep doing something like this until I die," she predicts. "At first I thought, *I'll keep going until I don't have the energy to do it anymore.* But the funny thing about that is, the more you serve other people, the more energy you have to do it. Then I thought, *I'll do it until I get tired of doing it.* But every day is a new adventure, so I don't get tired of doing it."

Some people retire from their careers and face a sense of aimlessness and lack of purpose. Not Karen. She awakens each day full of energy, ready to nudge the world in a positive direction. "As long as I'm breathing," she declares, "I'll keep striving to improve the lives of those who need help the most."

181

EPILOGUE

We sat cross-legged on embroidered carpets in a vast, ornate room filled with the voices of fifty nuns chanting at the Sangchen Dorje Laundrup Choeling nunnery near Thimpu, Bhutan. We arrived around 6:30 a.m., just as the morning sun started to filter in through the windows high above, illuminating those in the room against the dawn chill. The air smelled like incense and burning yak butter candles. It was how the morning of my 60th birthday started.

The nuns chanted well-known stories of Buddha, as well as the Sanskrit mantra *Om Mani Padme Hum* over and over. Occasionally they paused on cue to bang drums, hit cymbals, and blow giant horns—a cacophony of music, noise, and otherworldly sounds emanating from this holy place.

As I gazed across the room of serene faces, I had a chance to reflect upon where I had come from, where I might be going, as well as the meaning of my life. Michelle and I, as part of a Spirit Tours group from Northern California, felt humbled and a bit like intruders at times, though the nuns welcomed us warmly in the cold.

I imagined, like some sort of personal joke, that they were celebrating my milestone day with prayers sent upward and toward the giant Buddhas, statues, and carvings in the room. But of course, they weren't. If I was at home, I might be lamenting the day as my fifties ended. After all, I was no longer on the "back-nine," but had just a few holes left to make a mark.

Instead, my fellow travelers and I were filled with love, joy, peace, and a serenity that is so hard to find in the news-filled world of CNN, Facebook, and email. For many of us, it was a transcendent time that was not just a highlight of the trip, but a landmark experience in our lives that we would long remember.

During the day, we attended a local party in my honor. Okay, it was not in *my* honor— it was the Punakha Tsechu festival. But I could pretend that all the people in attendance were celebrating my milestone day. What I saw in a much broader sense was joy, happiness, and communal coming-together with costumes, music, and love for each other.

After an amazing day enjoying the colorful Buddhist festival, we returned after dinner to the relative warmth of the homestead where we were staying. To my surprise, our local guide, Tsering, had arranged for a chocolate birthday cake to be driven in from the nearest large town around three hours away. Newfound friends and strangers alike sang happy birthday as I blew out the candles and made my secret wish.

The next morning, before we chanted as a group, I had the opportunity to read an essay by Robert N. Test entitled "To Remember Me," which reflects on the end of life. It includes the lines:

> If you must bury something, let it be my faults, my
> weaknesses and all my prejudice against my fellow

man.

Give my sins to the devil.

Give my soul to God.

If, by chance, you wish to remember me, do it with
a kind deed or word to someone who needs you.

If you do all I have asked, I will live forever.

There was hardly a dry eye in the group, including mine.
It was a watershed experience to be in Bhutan during my
birthday week, and to hear what friends, colleagues, and
family had to say about my life. Michelle surprised me with
a lovely video she had created, which went through my life
in photos. These events, combined with the final writings for
this book, made me take stock of what I'd done with my life,
and what was yet left to be done.

185 —

A couple weeks later, I ran the Sundown Marathon here
in Singapore, a race that literally starts at midnight. I finished and received the finishers' medal for what was my
forty-ninth marathon—after the age of forty-five—and my
sixteenth straight year of running and completing a marathon or longer.

In some ways, that particular Sundown Marathon was
one of the hardest marathons of my life. Maybe it was the
heat and humidity, or perhaps I had not done enough training. Running in the middle of the night probably did not
help, but I also could not help thinking that maybe the real
issue was age.

As much as my mind (and probably yours also) thinks of myself as a much younger version of who I am today, time does march on. Together, we can accept this and make changes by living a healthier lifestyle and counter-balancing as much as we can.

A month later, I was fortunate enough to climb another mountain, this time with colleagues and partners in Taiwan. Jade Mountain (or YuShan in the English transliteration for the Taiwanese characters) is around thirteen thousand feet high and sits in the middle of the island. We were able to summit at 5:00 a.m. and see the explosion of stars in the sky turn into a glorious sunrise over the surrounding peaks and mountains.

Though there were no crampons or carabiners involved, it was a difficult climb over and around rocks and boulders during what seemed like a never-ending trek to get to the peak. I had forgotten how satisfying a climb could be and how the difficulties of getting to the top made it that much more worthwhile. During the climb, we heard about the death near Everest of Ulli Steck, the world-famous speed climber, which made me appreciate again how perilous aclimbing can be and how lucky I was—along with accomplished guides and fellow climbers—to be alive today.

It is indeed very difficult to live our lives in balance, endure life's sacrifices, mindfully ponder what our legacy will be, and face what lies ahead. The process has been extremely meaningful as I've undertaken to create, write, review, and edit this book. It turns out—not surprising to me—that I was actually coaching *myself* as I wrote. Like you, I desire deeply to continue to put my own passions into purpose, my intentions into actions—all the while coping with my fears and anxieties.

We don't know what our future holds, dear reader. Michelle and I have big dreams for what we want to do when we return from Singapore to the U.S.—but we also have many uncertainties about where we'll live, what our professions will be, and what we want to accomplish. And we truly want to reach beyond and outside ourselves—to somehow leave the world in a better place when we're no longer here. Our further hope, then, is that our kids and grandkids will carry on whatever legacy we leave.

I do know we are both continually inspired by others and the obstacles they have had to overcome, the heartbreaks they've endured, and the magical things they have been able to accomplish. We know we live in an uncertain world, both politically and economically, but we're increasingly confident and optimistic that basic human goodness will shine through in little and big ways—both globally and locally in the towns we are a part of.

187 —

We will be praying and rooting for all who read this book. When we say we are on the life-journey with you, we mean that forever we will be figuratively roped-up as we all climb our next mountains.

MITCH LEWIS

Singapore

ACKNOWLEDGMENTS

This book took much longer and was much harder to write than my first one. It's one thing to tell *my own* story; it is more difficult to tell another person's—to be able to tell their story with sensitivity, honesty, and conciseness. For this I have to credit my co-writer, Keith Wall. He was able to take long interviews and background material and craft it into inspiring profiles on the challenges overcome—and goals achieved—by our cast of contributors. As always, I appreciate Keith's support and guidance in helping me to become a better writer in the process.

Publishing a book includes a team of professionals who are dedicated to the cause and committed to the project. Gene and the Peak Teams/Up2Speed crew (including Tom and Tom's support) worked tirelessly to produce "handimation" video material and chapter graphics to illustrate our concepts in a compelling way.

Mario and the local media team at EastSide Mafia created the new website YourPersonalEverest.com and helped put together an integrated marketing plan for social promotion. Kyle Duncan did an outstanding job of copyediting our finished manuscript. Brent Nims at Nims Media came in late to do the amazing cover design, typesetting, and production work—a significant task from faraway Colorado.

I also want to acknowledge and thank all of our contributors: Aidan, Susan, Miha, Robin, Richard, Deborah, Alf, and Karen. Each one of them is like you and me: ordinary people trying to make it in the world and leave their mark in some significant way. Indeed, they all have pursued their passion with purpose, while encountering many obstacles along the way. But they have persevered toward greatness, while never being satisfied with where they are. I know they would also want to thank their spouses, partners, children, and parents for their support and love during their lives.

On the subject of support, I recently counted all the direct bosses I've had in my career so far and the number is around thirty-five, going back to my earliest days in telesales and AT&T, to my current position in Singapore. I've been so fortunate to work for men and women of all ages and nationalities, of many different styles of leadership, and from a number of diverse countries and states.

I can honestly say that I have learned from all of them; their wisdom and experience has helped me develop and grow, and hopefully helped me provide some of the same leadership, guidance, and support to my own teams. Like everyone, I've made professional missteps, mistakes, and mismanagement moves, but I've tried to learn from my errors and to appreciate the patience and feedback from my leaders, peers, and teams.

Life is incomplete if we cannot laugh at our circumstances—and laugh at ourselves even more. We need people around us who call us on our crap and allow us to be ourselves in the moment. While in Singapore, I've become part of a golf league team called the Putt Pirates. These folks are all expats like me from the U.S., U.K., Australia, and South Africa. We compete individually, and as a team, in a Monday-night after-work golf league at a well-lit local course. We all work in several different industries and companies, some with spouses and children, but we share a common love and frustration for the game. To my mates: Jack, Shaun, Morgan, Tom, Brett, Chris, Patrick, and our captain, aptly named Seven. Thank you for the fun, competition, and joy, and for being such good friends on and off the course.

In late 2016, I decided to make some personal improvement changes and know I needed some help to do so. Tom Imanishi from Virgin Active in Singapore has been the best personal trainer I've had the honor to work with. He pushes me extremely hard in strength and flexibility training, and he's in tune with my aging body. Thanks, Tom, for helping me get back some of my climbing and running abilities.

191

Having been frustrated with my short-game skills in golf, I also enlisted a swing coach, Nigel Bark, who has helped change my swing and make me more consistent in a game that is, by its nature, inconsistent. He's worked with me (and others on our team) on many aspects designed to help me get a little bit better over time.

It's not easy being away from our families and hometown friends while on assignment. Our children Jeremy, Nick, Jessica, Vincent, and Sadie continue to inspire us with their drive and ambition, with the struggles they've overcome, and the life values they demonstrate. We're thankful for technology that allows us to call and FaceTime, but it's not the same being nearly ten thousand miles away with time zone differences to overcome. We're grateful for reliable airlines that can whisk us to family in a day so we can experience hugs and kisses that are impossible over an iPhone.

It has been so special to see the parents that Jeremy and Carrie have become with Clara Marie; it's been a delight to watch Eric and Jessica manage their clan of Leah, Kailea, Ella, and Jackson while looking after their Grandma Jo, and keeping their faith. As Jessica says, "Blended, not shaken." Indeed.

Finally, with my own parents deceased for some time, I love that Michelle's parents, Nancy and Jess, have "adopted" me into their own family and insist on me calling them Mom and Dad. Having not grown up in a large family, I know that my own mom and dad would have loved their large family dinners and outings, and the non-stop overlapping conversations and love that is always visible.

Saving the best for last, this book would not have been possible without my loving wife, Michelle. Our late-night patio talks about family, politics, work, and life became the genesis for what is between the covers here. We had some truly amazing collaboration sessions where we brainstormed and hashed out the overall chapters, concepts, and key points. When I talk about being "roped-up together," I can think of no other perfect example than Michelle and me—working together and debating with love. We are of one mindset for the world we want to see, and the part we want to play in contributing to help change that world—while giving back, one person at a time.

NOTES

Prologue

1. Paul Kalanithi, *When Breath Becomes Air* (New York: Random House, 2016).

Chapter 1

1. J. D. Salinger, *The Catcher in the Rye* (New York: Little, Brown, 1951).

Chapter 3

1. David Whyte, *Crossing the Unknown Sea: Work as a Pilgrimage of Identity* (New York: Riverhead Books, 2002).

2. Shannon Adler, *300 Questions to Ask Your Parents Before it's Too Late* (Bountiful, UT: Horizon Publishers, 2011).

Chapter 7

1. Bruce Springsteen, "Thunder Road," Columbia Records, 1975.

2. Nickelback, "If Today was Your Last Day," Roadrunner Records, 2008.

Chapter 9

1. Carl Sagan, *The Demon-Haunted World: Science as a Candle in the Dark.* (New York: Ballantine Books, 1995).

Chapter 11

1. Ektarina Walter, *Forbes* Magazine, December 30, 2013.

2. Sidney Piburn, *The Dalai Lama: A Policy of Kindness*, p. 96 (Delhi, India: Motilal Banarsidass, 2002).

3. https://blogs.nasa.gov/spacex/2016/04.

Chapter 13

1. http://www.smh.com.au/good-weekend/how-filmmaker-jennifer-peedom-captured-everests-darkest-day-20160226-gn4xrl.html.

Chapter 15

1. https://archive.org/details/sermonsofchristm00evan.